Fred & Me

VICTOR BIBBY

www.raubgold.com

ISBN: 978-1-922409-99-7
Published by Vivid Publishing
A division of Fontaine Publishing Group
P.O. Box 948, Fremantle
Western Australia 6959
www.vividpublishing.com.au

A catalogue record for this book is available from the National Library of Australia

Cover design and typesetting:
Insomnia Design (www.insomniadesign.com.au)

ACKNOWLEDGEMENTS

I wondered about who to acknowledge in this very personal account of my father and me. Perhaps first, my family, for putting up with my persistent tendency throughout to ask questions of some and at the same time seek isolation. I know now, after this my second and probably last book, that writing is a solitary occupation. Also to the Anglican Church for its cooperation in allowing me access to its files and photographic archive, and those so-important personal diaries. Given the publicity of this particular subject matter, it was brave of them to do so. Thanks must also go to my editor, Christina Houen, for controlling my speculative imagination and dealing with my penchant for detail. There were many gaps to fill in this duo story, but enough is there to express what I wished to say. One comment I had in the making of this story is I say little about my mother, but this book is about my father after all, but she is always there though like the ghostly image on the page at the beginning of this book.

The cover for this book is a still from a compilation of amateur films made by Canon Richard Hamilton, the Rector of St Marys, who I mention in this book. It is from the very late 40s, not long before we arrived. In fact, some of the colour footage may even be later. It is reproduced with the permission of the Library Board of Western Australia. I recommend this evocative film archive to the reader which can be viewed at:
http://catalogue.slwa.wa.gov.au/record=b1424558~S2#.Uo7DRSeaaIA

CONTENTS

1

OPENING WORDS

Around noon, one of those blazing hot summer days you get in Perth; a day when the heat seems to weld your feet to the pavement. Any cooling 'Fremantle Doctor' was still many hours away. A slight and unimposing youth, less streetwise than most at his age, stepped alone through the coolness of a fortress-like portal, a sandstone relic of Western Australia's independent military past, pre-federation – the army recruiting office at Swan Barracks on Francis Street. Its aged weatherworn façade and grim look reminded him of another building – Waylen House, of similar Victorian architecture, where he had put his head down for most of the last nine years of his life, a boy learning to become a man.

It was January 6 1958; in December he had turned sixteen. He had come to Australia from England nearly ten years ago, but looked and spoke like a local. His only image of any army came from comic strips of supposed invaders from the north to this, his newly adopted country. Although this was the country of his father, he did not know that then, and it would take a long time before he did. He had worn a uniform before, but it was usually ill-fitting, pre-worn, and had Sea Scouts emblazoned on the chest. He liked the idea of wearing one again. He was not nervous, as he was used to authority, standing in lines, usually two by two, responding to shouted orders. He was also used to regular punishment for any misdemeanour, sometimes corporal, administered with a strap, slap, and on occasion, a rod, wielded by the man who had been in charge of his destiny for the past nine years. He had grown up with all of that since his young life changed when he arrived in Australia at the age of seven. He had a sense of humour, though, and saw that early part of his life as one of great expectations, a belief that he would hold all his life, that what was to come had to be better than his life so far.

He came to this portal to start the next part of his life, not to escape that early life, or on a whim, seeking adventure, although that was part of it. He had hoped to keep going to school, but his father's money had run out now. Used up, he thought then, by his older brothers; his sister was left out of that equation as girls' careers didn't matter then. But he knew nothing then of the real reason for all of that, and how his brothers and sister were being left behind. The army was not a career he had chosen consciously; others had done that for him. From now on, though, his fate would be his choice. In part, he was there because he had to leave the care he had known for his young days. His guardians, the State and the Anglican Church who had cared for him, were not paying for his keep any longer, because he had turned sixteen.

A letter addressed to his father from the army had arrived, summoning him to this appointment. It had his father's initials wrong, a hint of many bureaucratic errors regarding his father that he would encounter much later. He had not seen that letter, and would not, until some sixty plus years later. Reading it then made him laugh. It said to bring your lunch, and he thought back to school lunches arriving in a battered tin box conveyed by a yellow van. Although addressed to his father, it had been sent to the people at Swan Homes, whose care he had been in for the past nine years. He knew now it had all been pre-arranged, and the Swan Homes had called it a 'scholarship' with the army. Well, that was one way to describe putting on a uniform for nine years with a starting pay of seven pounds a week and full board and living, dormitory style again, but in huts with three hundred or so others around his age. All there to learn a trade or play a trumpet in a band, as well as how to march, shoot a 303 rifle, and use a bayonet. It was the army, though who would complete his High School education enabling him to go on to tertiary studies later, so it was a type of scholarship after all.

He had spent his adolescence at Swan, which was run by a Mr Peterkin, a figure who had loomed large in more ways than one in his life. Some, mainly the newspapers of the time, called it an orphanage, but only a few orphans were there. They were mostly kids with one or two parents from broken homes and lives, and like him, from annual intakes of English child migrants from similar situations. His years at Swan were passed in a spartan, sometimes harsh, at times lonely place, despite all those kids around him. Although he had three siblings there during that time, they were older; the eldest by five years was his brother Don. He knew little of them, what they were doing or how they felt; that was the nature of the place. They had already left and were like strangers to him, among the many others from Swan.

But he had made some friends and had seen the humour of the place more than the worst of it. So, he was well prepared for what was to come in army life. The discipline that would come with it would be like water off a duck's back. He had no qualms about this military future and was leaving nothing behind he really cared about. To him it was just like leaving one institution for another.

He mainly recalled the good times and the happy moments he had in those years. He had a few reliable friends forged through a childhood of survival of the fittest. No significant possessions, except a broken but still useful penknife and a bag of worn marbles, the blue cats-eye his favourite taw, but there would be no use for marbles where he was going. He carried little with him when he left except what he stood up in; his old high school long pants and a white shirt, a change of clothes in a canvas bag. His suitcase, the one he arrived in Australia with, which contained little but memories of himself as a younger child, long gone. To replace it at the end of this journey, he would get a kitbag full of uniforms, with a complete wardrobe, even a set of civvies, they had told him. He would soon find out it wasn't a set of civvies you would want to 'hang out' in with 'mods' or rock and roll fans, in those wonderful swinging sixties about to come. They did not teach you much about the world at Swan, even less about those who could break your heart, as he would find out soon enough. But he knew about blue suede shoes and rock and roll. He was a carefree adolescent, responsible to no one but himself, with ties to no-one on his way to Melbourne; it might as well have been another country again as far as he knew or cared.

This youth was me, and Fred was my father. I looked like a youth, not like a young man of an age to join the army. I imagine I looked like Fred when he signed up at the same age, but I knew nothing about that event and his life then. I was a pom from Essex now turned into an Aussie, or so I thought. Looking at that letter from the army now and the files that came with it, I cannot recall how my choice of a military career came about. My only firm memory about what I wanted to do as a career was that I liked to draw. One of my early Australian school reports says I was artistic and should be given the tools to foster that. Some teacher saw something in my drawings when I was eight or so, but that advice would fall on deaf ears of course; we were all treated the same at Swan. I have always liked to listen to music, and an early memory in England of pretending to conduct an orchestra at my English grandparents' home stays with me; there are only a couple of other short memories of that time. I would always remain a listener to music. I really wanted to be an architect, like one friend from Swan. He was a year older than me and had already left for a career as a cadet trainee in the Public Works Department of the Western Australian Government. However, there would be no arts and drawing in my future career.

I could enlist at such a young age because it was not for war as it had been for Fred; he said he was much older, at a time when people would look the other way and didn't ask for certificates. I enlisted for an apprenticeship like any other, but one undertaken in uniform. And of course, my documents and certificate of birth were all in order, I know now, unlike Fred's, as I later found out. The State, who had held my future in a tight fist for the past nine years, had made sure of that. Fred's father was born in Barkers Creek, near Castlemaine, Victoria, Australia, and Fred had enlisted in St Arnaud in 1915. Because his first marriage was in England and his second, to my mother Daphne, also in England, where I was born, I would find much later that I was considered not Australian enough and would have to be 'naturalised' to serve my country overseas. But that did not seem to matter to the Australian Army in January 1958.

I didn't see my birth certificate until much later in life. It would turn up in the State files obtained by my eldest brother Don; much of this story could not have been written if he hadn't taken that step. I don't know what prompted him at the time, but maybe it was a premonition, as he had not much longer to live. It was when Margaret Humphrey blew the whistle on child migration loud enough for people to take notice. I read her book and the stories by others, watched the films and television shows. But that was a time when I didn't look back and ask questions, like so many; I was just getting on with my life.

I am pretty sure Don met Margaret in Perth one time, as

a copy of her book, *Empty Cradles,* had passed down to my daughter with a telltale mark on a certain page. But I have no idea what he felt about it all. He was working in welfare at the time of his death in 2004. He had found a past friend from Swan days as a loyal and seemingly ideal partner and settled down in North Perth. And on the rare times we met, he seemed to always have around him a family, but not his own; maybe he saw something of himself in them, people with gaps in their lives that he tried to fill. He spent the least time at Swan of the four of us, but maybe he had an experience there that set him apart from those who wanted a family later on. Anyway, he might have worked the system, being an insider so to speak, to get the files on us, I mean. So, thank you Don!

Turning sixteen in December 1957 meant I had ceased to be a ward of the State, and Swan had sorted out my future. So, I had to go somewhere else to live while waiting to be recruited, and it was with Fred, who was lodging at 36A St Georges Terrace, Perth. I know this because it was the address on my application to join the army, which Fred had filled in for me. I can still vaguely remember the place, one of a couple of detached, wooden, one-room cabins in the grounds of a large house in a somewhat prestigious location. I now know who it belonged to, a lady well known in Perth at the time, who took in boarders. The house was alongside the Presbyterian Church, which is still there, so all above board, but lodgings for single men only. In writing this story, I found out why he was there, and I see now it fits his circumstances at the time. He had been paying for my brother's and Don's education at the prestigious Guildford Grammar School, and later had him and my sister and other brother in his care after they left Swan. So, being of no skilled trade or profession and working as a barman then, he might have found life hard.

This was about five years after he had left a life at sea, where he had reached the lofty heights of smoking-room steward. He left his ship at Fremantle in August 1952 with two other crew, a British stowaway, three cats and one budgerigar, the record states. I have a memory from that recruitment time of him cooking a roast dinner in one of those old metal gas stoves with an oven, and with the pudding mix underneath the roasting meat. That pudding tasted like heaven, unlike anything I had eaten before. I would learn where he got that culinary skill much later in my life, and it wouldn't be until I got married that I would taste that heaven again. I did not know then why Fred chose to live at such an auspicious address in such rustic accommodation. But from what I have learned about him now, I can imagine how it came to be, and why he might have chosen to live in such a well-known street in Perth.

My journey east was by train through Kalgoorlie, which I don't think I knew existed till then. My memory of the geography we were taught then is only of how Empire-red the world was. Kalgoorlie and that plain were a completely new world for me, just like the eastern states. I would make that return train journey twice a year for the next three, so

I would get to know Kalgoorlie and what was beyond and in between very well. I travelled with a small group of what was called the 'Thirteenth' intake to the Army Apprentices School at Balcombe on Port Phillip Bay in Victoria. Fred had to sign my enlistment papers, as a parent's consent was needed; he never really played that part, although the State seemed to think he did. I only stayed with him a few days at the time of my enlistment and I do not remember him being present at the Barracks when I signed up. My memory of those last days before and after I left Swan is not clear. At least I have all the records, so I know now why it all happened. Although I knew Fred then, it was not in the way a son in a normal family would.

I did not know then that I was repeating what he had done at the same age, almost to the day, in St Arnaud in 1915. I wonder now if he might have had a flashback of that time and remembered his regimental number when he signed my papers. His number was 1915 and I think now, did Fred see that as a lucky number? Perhaps it was, from what happened to him in his war. He told me nothing about that then, nor what had happened to him afterwards and throughout his life. But I know a lot more about that now, although not all, I'm sure! Fred enlisted by his own choice, not like me, with a motivation different than any I had. He probably saw it as chance to get away from what he saw in front of him. Whereas I wanted to go somewhere new and as far away from Swan as I could.

Fred had no father then, but was from a loving family

with a mother and two brothers, who lived comfortably in a large established home in the bosom of a surrounding, extended, successful and well-known family in a large country town. So, he was leaving something much more important behind than just one or two close friends. When I compare my signature on my enlistment papers with his, he had signed his attestation papers with a neater and more confident-looking signature than mine. His has a small flourish, which might suggest he had had a good education. From what I know now, more likely it was because he thought he was something else other than just a boy recently finished high school and had other ideas about his destiny in life. At sixteen plus a couple of months, he could not have been much taller than me, or much different than I do in my enlistment photograph seen in this book. They did not look closely at his age then or ask for credentials; they just wanted volunteers to go to Europe as fodder for the guns and help their king fight the Hun. They didn't question his age, just as my recruitment Sergeant ignored my wonky vision, which would haunt me in later life. Young men then saw the war as the 'grand adventure.' How wrong they were; it would not be long before Fred found that out. If that was not enough for him, there was more after that, just as adventurous, if not as dangerous.

Fred's story as I tell it here is from his birth in Malaya – only briefly but enough to establish the home he came from – to when he enlisted, his military career, and the re-invention of himself and return to what he really was. His war was short, but its impact on his life great. His time afterwards in England, marriage, 'consorting' with the brother-in-law of the richest Maharajah in India, and upsetting the India Office, divorce, marriage to my mother Daphne, and final humble return to his home country, were episodes in a chequered career. So this is really his part-biography, but it is the best part.

For me, I tell why I came to Australia from England in 1949, and his role in that, aside from being my father of course. He had a hand in what I became in life because, I believe now, we were alike in many ways. He would appear from time to time during my youth, more regular than Santa Claus, with gifts. So, in a way, he did understand something about family and its obligations – later in his life, anyway. I couldn't ignore the many coincidences and the serendipitous nature of how we both started out on life's adventure, that first independent step that made us what we were to become. From what I learnt about him, we might have had similar dreams. I tell them together because I want my children, and theirs, to know his story and the early part of mine as an affirmation of where they came from.

This story is only a vignette of Fred's life. I did not know him personally or live with him for any significant period, and I could count on one hand our meetings as I grew up. He left no diary or journal and told me nothing about his earlier life on the odd occasion when we met, as I grew into a young man. What his second wife Daphne said about him is little and not that kind; I will deal with that as his story unfolds. What I found out is almost purely from the public records, where, fortunately, he is mentioned occasionally but not always kindly, and some family anecdotes handed down. What I found out about him and the correspondence with events in my own life was so fascinating it drove me to write this 'duo story.' I end these opening words by saying that, although the memory of my life at Swan has faded, it is mostly the truth. Some of the names I mention in this story are real, and some are made up because I felt it best that way. Either way, I hope that, if those who chance to read it recognise themselves, they are not offended, and will laugh rather than feel sorry about it all. I will tell it has it happened!

2

FRED AT ST ARNAUD

Fred was always a shadowy figure in my life, as I hardly knew him and my memory of him is scant. But I know more about him now that he is not here than I ever did when he was. As for what type of person he was, I can only go to the records, for the most part. Adding to that are some hints like small notes on official forms, and his signature at an early age; all tell me that sometimes he might have wanted to be someone other than he became. His is, in a way, a poignant story. From the brief official accounts of his life, he appears to have striven to become someone important, to exceed the circumstances he found himself in, and he wanted to be liked by all he met. What clearly stands out from all of that is that he had a certain bonhomie that seemed always to be his style. I believe it was this that shaped him throughout his life. I will try to draw a picture of his childhood. For that, I have to digress somewhat into his family past.

Fred's story is also about the question of what might have been, when fate briefly opened for him a door to a very different life than the one that he finally had. The circumstances of his birth, his beginnings, were somewhat more exotic than for many. He had a large Australian family of uncles, aunts, and cousins, on both his father's and his mother's side. What he was told, or imagined, about his parents and his paternal grandfather, William Bibby, probably influenced him when, as a younger man, he did an extraordinary thing – and it wasn't signing up underage – that dramatically changed the direction of his life. It is the story I believe he was told that might have set him apart in some way. This exotic circumstance of his beginnings was something he would use in his plans to reinvent himself in a bold and extraordinary way.

Fred's father was Frederick Alfred Bibby and his mother, Annie Brain. Their story can be found in my book about William Bibby, Fred's grandfather. Annie came from an extended local farming family from St Arnaud, Victoria, but she was born near Geelong where I now live. They married in 1894.An article on the wedding appeared in the local newspaper, *The St Arnaud Mercury,* and the description gives a hint of Fred's gold mining ancestry, and perhaps underlines the prominence of the family connection in that community. The James in his name came from his mother's father. The Brain family were well known in that town. His father, Frederick Alfred, also came from an extended Australian mining family and was born in Castlemaine. This is what makes Fred's story intriguing – how and why did he end up in St Arnaud, where this story starts?

Fred's story starts at the end of the nineteenth century in early 1898, when his mother moved with his elder brother to Malaya, as it was called, to join his father, who worked at the goldmine in Raub. It was a time when the Empire focussed its attention on the East, and Singapore in particular. Where

Fred was born was under a British Colonial Government. The records of the arrival of his parents in Malaya show that he must have been conceived in St Arnaud. So, his mother travelled heavily pregnant; Fred had a twin, a situation with considerable risk then, given where they were headed. She was heading for a mining town in one of the most backward States, Pahang, with no roads, just pony tracks. There was no infrastructure and the nearest doctor was a day's travel by pony cart or horse. Malaya was called the Protected Malay States then. Of course, Fred was too young during his time there to bring back any memories of that life, but from the stories handed down by his immediate family later, when he was of an age to dream, it could well have influenced what he wanted to be in life.

Frederick James, or Fred, as he always called himself as far as I know, was born on August 3 1898 in Kuala Lumpur, Selangor, capital of the Protected Malay States. Fred would always claim he was born in Singapore, which to him as a young man, was probably a more exotic and well-known place, but he was definitely born in Kuala Lumpur. The twins' birth was published on August 4 of that year in the *Malay Mail,* the main local daily newspaper then. His mother might have told him of her journey across a four-thousand-foot mountain range by pony cart to the east, some twenty miles as the crow flies. Then down through to Kuala Kubu, a small town where the steam train to Kuala Lumpur terminated. The British had brought the railway early to that part of the Malay States. The road ran from Raub where the family lived at the gold mine started by his grandfather. It traced a tortuous path with many switchbacks across Frasers Gap, as it is still called. The road had only been opened the year before. After his birth, with his mother and twin brother, he went back the same way. Such stories might have been the stuff for Fred's fertile imagination.

No birth certificate has surfaced, but I suspect an official record survives, probably in some colonial archive somewhere, in England rather than Australia, since Malaya was under English control when Fred was born. He certainly did not have one throughout his life, judging by what he told everybody about when and where he was born. His twin brother's Melbourne family told me that their grandfather, who lived to his nineties, always lamented that he did not have one. So throughout his life, this other twin also managed without one. This twin, Arthur Edward, never left Australia after returning from Malaya with Fred. It was Arthur and his family I would stay with occasionally on leave from Balcombe, the Army Apprentices School, after leaving Swan. But I did not know then the significance of who he was, or where he was born.

For Fred, however, throughout the medical and military records and up until his death, his date and place of birth is consistently given as Singapore. It is surprising he got through life well enough without a certificate, particularly when he signed up. It is only much later in Australia, in his later medical repatriation records, that the actual year of his birth, 1898, appears, but the place of birth is never changed from Singapore. However, Singapore and some other date seemed to have become facts for him, as both are repeatedly given throughout his life as different. It was the beginning of the life of Fred as he saw it, and he made it up, it seems, as the occasion called for. This discrepancy between what some of the records say about him and what he said contribute to his mystery.

His father, Frederick Alfred, was the third son of William Bibby. William was from Liverpool, England, and found his first success in the goldfields of Victoria. He would make a name for himself in his own way, particularly in Pahang and Singapore. Of all of William's six sons, Frederick Alfred was the one who left home very early to seek his fortune elsewhere when the family seemed to be settled in Castlemaine, although the father was often absent on his gold ventures. Frederick Alfred was not an engineer like his father. From what I found out about him, he seemed to have no trade, and was variously in charge of the boilers or working as an amalgamator, one who sorts the crushed ore as it comes out of the stamps or crushing mill onto tables at his father's gold mine at Raub, at the time of Fred's birth. He would have learnt such skills from his father or his father's cohorts. Frederick's family had been a typical gold mining family of their time – family at home with the father away finding his fortune. But a father who always came home and kept the family together.

Frederick Alfred's father William first went to Maldon and took out a mining lease in Wattle Gully, went bankrupt like many, moved around the Castlemaine district and in a number of other gold rush places, as far north as northwest Queensland, always working in gold mining, but finally made his fortune crushing ore. No matter where he went, he always returned and looked after his family. It's likely that this story of William was the source of much of Fred's imaginings then, and later in his life. William died in Kuala Lumpur in May 1900. Except for Fred's uncle, Arthur Hector, one of four sons who stayed to make a life in Malaya, they all returned to Melbourne within a year.

All of that is another tale I have already told in *William's Story*. Fred and his twin brother Arthur left Raub for St Arnaud with their mother in late 1900 to join his older brother William Raub and await the return of their father. His older brother had been taken to Australia earlier by an aunt. A lack of education facilities at Raub was the reason for the family's return to Australia. *William's Story* relates how Fred's father died suddenly at Raub in 1901. The description suggests it was acute dysentery. From what I found, the bond of love was very strong between Annie and Frederick. So, Fred knew no father, but his mother would likely have made sure he knew about him and his place in her life. His older brother, nearly five, wasn't old enough to be any kind of father figure, so he only had those male adults of the Brain farming family to look up to. Judging by what happened next, it seems unlikely he needed a father. So, Fred's life story really began in St Arnaud when he was three years old, not in the exotic East.

St Arnaud had gold at one time as well as grain, but the gold had long gone when Fred returned with his brother and mother in 1900. It was gold that had brought his father to St Arnaud. The town had become a rural centre servicing the farmers and those miners who stayed and turned to growing wheat. Some of those farmers, including his mother's father, James Brain, had dabbled with gold to help pay the bills, but by Fred's return, farming was where the living was made. The country there is still wheat plains. In the summer it is dry and hot, and when you look west, the plains seem to be endless. The family farm lay where the plains begin and the road to it bears the Brain family name. East, a short distance away, are the low hills where St Arnaud lay, by then a busy country town of some size. In the winter, the winds that scorched the summer earth turn bitterly cold, and at one time, in one of nature's weather freaks, they brought snow to the region that was so thick it hid the streets of the town.

The family were living on a prosperous farm owned by his mother's father at a place called Waterloo Plains, on the edge of what they call the Wimmera. The farm was called Everton, named so by his mother's father. There is still a farm there, and a Brains Road off the Wimmera Highway that runs west. A ghostly and evocative hearth and some steps leading nowhere remain where the old homestead stood, nudging at farm buildings and an outhouse adjacent to the new place. This property was well known in the area, and figured regularly in the local paper with news about the family and what they were doing. So, the Brain family's

St Arnaud history is well documented in the local papers. We were described as good settler stock when we migrated from England, as was Fred's family on both sides. Fred's Australian settler roots were well founded. The Brains farm was well known and called a 'model farm' in the press. Other members of the family owned a hotel, a hardware store, and a grocery store at various times. Fred's father leased the Brain-owned grocery store when his luck with easy gold ran out in the early 1890s, and there, in 1892, he met Fred's mother. The same building that was the grocery store is now a house, as I found when I was researching Fred's great grandfather William's gold story.

Picturing Fred in those formative years after he returned to St Arnaud, I start with seeing a boy from around seven, the age when I arrived at Coogee. The photographs of them from that time show they were well-fed and well-dressed, certainly not living like urchins. Not like that one of me and my brothers and sister in our very early years in England. As I have no real family life to remember, I can only imagine what it was like for Fred living with his mother and two other brothers, the older one, maybe, with memories of Raub, bragging to his younger brothers and telling them stories of sultans, rajahs and amahs and rebellion. Food, I believe now, for a fertile young mind to create the imaginary world of an exotic life in the east that he would describe in letters later. Annie might have had dreams for them, as they all completed high school, so it was clear she did not want them to be farmers. Records show they all attended Beazleys

Bridge primary school. Although I found no attendance records, I know they went to that school, as Fred's and his brother William Raub's names appear on the WWI memorial just across the road from the site of the school. In the 1900s, it might have been a thriving community, but today there is a public hall and little else. Today, when I look at the markers and plaques where the school was, I wonder if Fred ever knew this later in his life. But I don't think he ever returned.

The site is only a short distance south of the Everton farm, after the turnoff from the Wimmera Highway junction onto what is now called the Sunraysia Highway that runs south to Ballarat, where an uncle, Harry was living at that time after he had also left Raub. The school was only some three kilometres away. Walking that distance would have been usual in those days; it's only a little further than the distance I walked to school from Swan. But, given the prosperity of the farm, it's likely they went by pony cart or similar, or even rode horses. From what I know now of Fred, I have difficulty imagining him in the saddle, even at that age. The school's similarity to my primary school when I arrived at Swan gave me an unexpected connection to Fred when I saw its images. What his grades were are lost to history, but he had an energetic mind, as we will see, and may have found school much as I did when I went to Swan. My school was set in country something like his, although much greener, and there were grapevines instead of grain fields So, I began to see, in Fred's childhood, similarities with mine. But I don't think he had dust between his toes or got the cold 'cuts' I got on my feet; I reckon he would have mostly worn boots of some kind.

That primary school must have been well built, as it was transported to St Arnaud in 1948 to supplement the primary school there. It is now the changing room for the children enacting the period-costumed schools at Sovereign Hill in Ballarat, having been transported there intact in 1982. So, unlike my first Swan primary school, which is long gone, its life goes on well after Fred, and if I go to Sovereign Hill and visit that building, I can stand in the same room where Fred sat and whiled away his early school hours dreaming of what he would do in life. The schoolhouse markers and the war memorial, along with what's left at the Brain farm, are the few tangible relics I have of his early life, to remind me that part of my roots lie here, not only in England. As he played around the farm, walked and rode to school with his siblings in those early school years, what young thoughts went through his mind? Thoughts, no doubt prompted by his mother's recollections of his father and tales of gold mines and natives and servants in a faraway exotic land of his early years. It's likely that Fred began his own dreams from that family story and the tales of gold in Australia and Malaya that were told by his mother and his elder brother, but he dreamed his own version of it.

Most of the children who came from families like Fred's went on to St Arnaud high school. His brothers, William Raub and Arthur Edward, can be found on the school rolls, but Fred's name is not there, for some reason. But he was there; his name appears on the honour roll that hangs in one of the assembly halls as serving in WWI, but Will's name, who also served, does not, strangely. I could not find any certificate, but by the timing of his subsequent enlistment, he should have completed his final year. No qualifications or certificates appeared among his meagre final possessions, yet that would not hold him back, as we shall see. I believe that he left school in that summer of December 1914 with something eating at his insides – that he was somehow meant for greater things than tilling the land. If that was in his mind, what else was there to do in St Arnaud but think of joining up? The trumpets of war beckoned with such attraction as an overseas 'adventure' in those times for a young boy on the verge of manhood. The country towns of Victoria, even the smallest, seemed to compete to enlist their youngest as well as not so young men, as the memorials to their service in every country town now show. To the young then, it was seen as an adventure and a chance to go overseas, and a patriotic duty, of course.

Unlike me, he had no letter telling him to turn up. Did he just walk into town from the farm, or skive off from school just to look when the recruiters came to town earlier? They would have been in St Arnaud from soon after August 1914, when the war preparations were announced. By December, he had finished school, as far as he was concerned, and when he took that fateful step into the local recruiting station, no doubt any ideas of further education were far from his mind. Whether he had the ability to continue his education is another matter, and I will never know now. Any advice from his mother, I expect, would have been about learning a skill or profession like his father; she may have thought he was destined for something else, considering what the rest of the family had achieved. Further schooling was over for him, though, when he took his oath in St Arnaud early in January the following year.

So how did this sixteen-year-old boy from St Arnaud in northwest Victoria, with no father, but living comfortably and clearly cared for by a well-established family, end up in England in the spring of 1916, a soldier discharged from the AIF a few weeks before his eighteenth birthday, and married to a woman almost twice his age? This period, from when he left St Arnaud in 1915 and turned up later in Australia in the early 1920s, was to be the defining period of how he would live his life. From then on, and after World War II, his world in England fell apart and he became, perhaps, what he truly was, just an ordinary bloke with dreams.

3

SIGNING UP

I asked myself, why did Fred leave the family nest when he had a secure future before him at home? In an early photograph, probably when the twins were just starting high school, the poses are standard for the period, but they tell a lot, especially the posture of his older brother William Raub, who was seated in front. Compared with a photo of their father when he first arrived at Raub, the older son is a spitting image in posture and looks. This led me to think that, as far as Annie's father was concerned, William might end up taking his father's place in St Arnaud and become a farmer. It was around this time that Annie's father bequeathed her eighty acres of the farmland, which might have seemed unusual for that time. Maybe it was because he expected her oldest son to carry on the family tradition.

However, I now think that may not have been the case. My older brother, who probably spent more time with Fred than any of us, told me a that Fred's maternal grandfather, James Brain, the model farmer, loomed large in his life and was perhaps a feared figure. My brother said Fred nearly always referenced him with a curse. At the end of his education, Fred put 'Farmer' as his occupation when he signed up; I suspect it meant nothing to him, as we will see. Was Fred seen as the chosen farmer of the three boys? Had his grandfather mapped out his future on the land with his mother, staying in St Arnaud? Given what happened in his life, I don't think he would have had a bar of life on the land – and I'm not demeaning farmers, I hasten to add. But this was probably the main reason he left so suddenly after just finishing high school. So, was that really the intention, that Fred, not his older brother William, should replace their lost father on the land while the other brothers followed their dreams? There would be no Bibby farm at St Arnaud, if that was the plan. The prospective farming son had flown the coop. Not long after, by 1920, Annie sold her block of land to another local farmer when she moved to Melbourne. The older son became a banker and Fred's twin became a chemist. Throughout his life, Fred kept the real reason he left home, and a lot of other things that happened to him in his early life, to himself. Having no father probably gave him a sense of independence that led him not to tell his mother what he planned. I believe that it was the family stories of gold in Malaya that made him look for his own pot of gold, and here was a golden opportunity. The fact that he was underage appeared not to matter to him, and perhaps that fear of his mother's father was what drove him to leave without telling anybody, as it would appear he might have.

His mother would soon know what he had done, whether he told her beforehand or not. His departure for Melbourne became local news. All who enlisted were announced in the local paper, as was Fred, but he had left by then. If he had known, Annie's father could have intervened, seeing the preferred farmer in the family about to walk out the door. They all would have known he was under the age for enlistment. St Arnaud was a small town, and the Brains were well known, as well as the name Bibby and its connection to the Malaya gold family. The word would have got out pretty quickly as to who had joined up in the patriotic fervour that prevailed then. She could have stopped him of course, judging by records of similar cases, but for some reason it did not happen. The older son, William Raub, would eventually enlist in 1916, and his name appeared in the local paper, even though he was not living in St Arnaud at the time. Interestingly for those times, Fred's twin Arthur would never serve. Maybe his mother stopped him from going, thinking two were a sufficient sacrifice.

So for whatever reason, at the same age and month as me, on January 9 1915, he came to a decision that would change his life, and signed up to serve in the AIF. The difference was that his step of enlisting was his alone, and mine was made by somebody else. So he went some fifteen kilometres, probably on his own, to St Arnaud, to the local drill hall. The big Anzac event was some months away, but the world war was well under way by that time. Did he know that he might end up, if accepted, in the Middle East, not Europe? I wonder if he took the chance to absent himself in the weeks leading up to enlistment and check out with his friends the recruiting place and where he would likely be sent. The 6^{th}Battalion, which I will just call the 6th, was the unit he was ultimately assigned to. He was part of the 5th Reinforcement, which had a roll of one-hundred and fifty-four names; two are shown as from St Arnaud, but they were not farmers. Recruits for the 6th were all from country Victoria, as it was the practice to keep recruits from states and their districts assigned to the same military unit. At this time, the 6th was not at Gallipoli, but training in Egypt, preparing for the expected desert campaign. They were part of the Middle East Expeditionary Force and not destined for Europe, which was the expectation of many; their true destination dismayed many of them, as some recorded in their written and other accounts. It seems France and Belgium were on the minds of most when they enlisted, like Fred probably. However, he may have thought he knew quite a lot about the east from his mother and eldest brother.

One other from St Arnaud, who signed up a few days before Fred, was a George Percy Lowe, who may not have attended the high school as he does not appear on the same high school Honour Roll. So, it is unlikely he knew Fred as a high school mate, although they were the same age. His enlistment papers state he was eighteen-and-a-half, the same as Fred. This shows Fred was not alone in lying about his age. Many did, if you look at the records. George would land at Anzac Cove a few days after Fred, stay throughout apparently without injury, and survive the Anzac evacuation, stay with the 6th, get wounded in France, and finally return to Australia in 1918. Their names appear in the newspaper together later. Another from St Arnaud was a Wilkie George Dowling, but he enlisted in Melbourne that same year in January. He called himself a labourer aged twenty-one. His birth record show he was born in 1895 so his age was pretty well on the mark. Wilkie would land together with Fred and his reinforcement group at Anzac Cove. So he must have known Fred at some time. Wilkie would survive Gallipoli without any recorded wound, and end up in France, but not with the 6th, and go missing in action. He finally returned home at the end of the war, I suppose you could say unscathed, but we all know now that may not be true. I would like to think they might have linked up with Fred, either of them, during their time in training or in Egypt and before their first big event together, but I cannot know if Fred knew these two in St Arnaud. Anyway, perhaps because they were of a different parish, Lowe and Dowling did not end up on the St Arnaud Anglican Church's WWI Honour Roll like Fred – another visible, long-lasting scrap of Fred's past I only found out about well after he died. So Fred appeared on two WWI Honour Rolls in St Arnaud as well as Beazleys Bridge, but there was not a whisper of this by him during his later life. Perhaps he wanted to put St Arnaud and all that early period out of his life altogether!

The minimum age was nineteen then and did not change to eighteen until June that year. The family photograph that was taken probably taken around about 1912 or 1913, when the twins had started high school for example, suggests he looked his age then, so how did he make it seem he was much older than he was only a few years later? The image he presented to a Major Gibbs who took his attestation might have been convincing enough, even putting aside the patriotic fervour of the times. Perhaps the need for many volunteers overshadowed all. It was a volunteer army then, and despite conscription referendums, as the casualties mounted throughout the war and the source of volunteers faltered, it would remain so. In his papers he stated he was "born in Singapore… near the town of Malacca." His high school geography seems amiss, as even in his time, they were distinctly different places; Malacca was on the Malay Peninsula about halfway between Singapore and Kuala Lumpur. The only connection with Malacca is Port Dickson, where his Uncle Charles would have passed on his way to the Negri Sembilan looking for gold in another Malay State, like his father William was already doing in Pahang. Was this the beginning of his story telling? Surely his mother told him he had been born in Kuala Lumpur.

I found it curious that the statement he was born in two separate places would end up on his attestation papers without a comment in the margin. I also found it curious that he did the same thing as his grandfather William did in England; as a young man not much older than he was, William went to the Crimean war, but unlike him, he served for a little longer, apparently unscathed. Did Fred know of that story from his mother? Again, the coincidence and serendipity of it makes me wonder to this day. Fred's invention would be repeated, and not just once, again and again. One should not judge him harshly though and maybe even salute this very young man from a country town with an imagination. His imagination would stand him in good stead later, but would also be his downfall.

His departure along with George Lowe and the others in his cohort was announced in the local newspaper, the *St Arnaud Mercury*, on Wednesday January 13, stating they had departed by train for Melbourne the same day – like me many years later, the same within a few days. Although the same age, I wasn't a real soldier then and would have to wait three years to be called a Private. Not Infantry like Fred, who was a Private on enlistment, ready to join his one hundred and fifty reinforcements and scattering of Boer War veterans and go off to war. With me were thirty-odd seniors from the earlier two-year classes returning from leave. Among them were some of the bullying types that you always find, not joshing and giving banter like Fred might have had, but of a more malicious kind I had not found at Swan. But I had been well prepared for that, and I could box. Our journey took five days; Fred's to Melbourne took a few hours.

So it all happened pretty quickly, and I find it hard to believe his mother did not know. Still, questions will always remain for me – how he achieved it, why he did it, and why his mother allowed him to do it? She surely knew the age limit; her eldest was squarely in that recruitment bracket. Recruits under nineteen needed parents' or guardians' consent to go overseas and he was also under the specified weight and chest measurement! Later correspondence between her and the army shows she that might have known all. The public view of his twin Arthur seems quite different. At a town social event in September 1915, Arthur is described as 'Master Bibby' in the local newspaper when participating in a Gymkhana. He was dressed as an Indian Prince, a telling role, and almost unbelievably prophetic in terms of what happens later with Fred.

4

GETTING READY FOR WAR

The reasons Fred went to war are shrouded in unanswerable questions. But what can be answered is what happened to him after he signed up. Fred was enlisted as the 5th Reinforcement for the 6th. What happened then can probably be accurately reconstructed from the record. I say probably, as in the record there is conflicting information in regard to some dates, and particularly the reason for his evacuation from Gallipoli and what happened afterwards when he was sent to England. However, with the help of war diarist C W Bean's chronicle, Austin's book on the 6th, *Rough as Bags,* official brigade and battalion war diaries, and many other personal accounts readily available, I can construct fairly accurately what was going on at Broadmeadows before they left and later in Egypt and the Dardanelles.

Using Bean's accounts and the war diaries, we can reconstruct what happened at Gallipoli when he landed at Anzac Cove. This short time at Anzac Cove and the events leading up to his evacuation to Malta is without doubt the key to all that happened later. His military and repatriation medical records and later archival material from England help to fill in the rest. But without any records from him and given the fact that he is not mentioned like some are in the actions described (he is only listed in the Battalion Nominal

Roll in Austin's book), some conjecture is still needed to fill in the obvious gaps. So, the story of what probably happened to him after he arrived in Melbourne is mostly fact supported by part construction. For that matter, this goes for his whole story until he turned up in Melbourne later in 1922 to visit, and then in late August 1952 in Perth, following us to stay in Australia. I have mostly left military terms undefined; they can be looked up in the many sources available these days.

Until they arrived in Egypt to join the 6th, Fred's 5th Reinforcement was commanded by a Major Peters. Peters might have appeared as a father figure to the younger recruits like Fred. He was well into his middle age, a Boer War veteran. Fred and the Major's paths would cross more than once later. The names of Fred's St Arnaud cohort that appeared in the local news on that fateful day of leaving were George Percy Lowe, Humphrey A.E., O'Grady T.J., Palmer C.J., and Watson W.H. These names were important to me, as they are human faces to the events happening around Fred. Only Lowe would join the 6th with Fred; the rest went to other units. Apart from Fred, who had called himself a farmer, they were all labourers except for Watson, who was a blacksmith who went to the Light Horse Regiment, not surprisingly. The average 'recorded age' of this group was eighteen. All would return after the war, some wounded.

They would have arrived at Spencer Street Station in Melbourne the same day. Then, I imagine with little delay, they went by a short local rail ride north to Broadmeadows.

Earlier, when Fred's original Victorian 6th assembled at Spencer Street, the practice was to form up and march part of the way through the city then march to Broadmeadows – another show of patriotic fervour. It is unlikely Fred was put through that by his time; but I wondered when I read it if they got a similar reaction as when we marched through Melbourne. I can recall assembling at the Domain in Melbourne, near Flinders Street station, as an army apprentice for a Coral Sea Battle march during my time at the Army Apprentices' School, probably in May 1959, the battle anniversary month. I still recall a shrill voice calling out as we marched down Swanston Street "Oh, they are so young, some are just kids" Well, we were only army apprentices, but you could take that as perhaps an echo from Fred's past!

We carried the same type of rifle Fred was issued, with bayonets fixed. Mine might have been a later generation, but it was the same basic Lee Enfield 303 with the same type of bayonet. I had no idea that day at the Domain that I would follow Fred's journey to England, though more directly, and not on my way to war. Also, like Fred, I would end up at Broadmeadows, but as a subaltern in the late 1960s, learning, among other things, to be an officer and gentleman. When I was there, it was a well-established camp with barracks, a workshop, an ordnance depot, and an officers' mess, where I stayed, of course. It was surrounded by housing, not by farming land like when Fred was there. It was where all the Victorian original battalions and their reinforcements that followed gathered for equipping and training prior to embarkation as part of the 2nd Brigade of the AIF.

What I stayed in would not have compared with Fred's accommodation; there were only tents in his time. Some, according to Austin, called it "something between a cattle yard and a ploughed field." The war was well and truly on in Europe by the time he arrived for training, but that main event, Gallipoli, was not that far away. His 6th was still in Egypt training for the assault on Anzac Cove. The 6th was among the early infantry units raised for the AIF for the First World War, and like the 5th, 7th and 8th, all Victorians; together, these battalions formed the 2nd Brigade. It was raised within a fortnight of the declaration of war in August 1914. These original or core battalions had embarked for Egypt just two months earlier. Austin's book gives a very detailed description of what took place at Broadmeadows. I will just give the highlights that might have applied to Fred.

At that time, the Australians had no experience with the type of warfare they were about to face. The Boer war threw up a body of experienced veterans and these, combined with the citizens' militia, would form the core of the officer corps and non-commissioned officers. The Second-in-Command of the 6th, Major George T. Bennett, would become its commander later; he was a veteran of that kind. I would serve under his namesake, a Major at officers' school, no relation, I think, but it made me stop and say to myself – so there it is again! There was also a citizens' militia who were infantry units from the various towns and cities that provided less experienced NCOs. Experienced soldiers such as NCOs, who were the heart of the training, were hard to find. Most had already departed with the main battalions. There was no training in trench warfare, and they did not even have an up-to-date manual on tactics. But they would learn the basics fast, likely treating it as a lark, not knowing anything about what they were going to face. What training they got was weapon drill and following orders, which was hard for some to accept, judging by some of their service records. Consequently, the training at Broadmeadows involved mainly skirmish practice, and of course, parades and drill, drill, and more drill, with a church parade every Sunday. Uniforms were in still in short supply, according to Austin, particularly the ubiquitous 'slouch hat.'

They were issued with an identification disc, which Austin describes as "22 gauge aluminium, and about the size of a penny"; this was sewn into the lining of the left hand bottom of a soldier's tunic. I wonder about whether they got one, a tunic that is, as although they were assigned to go to the 6th, they weren't actually in that unit yet. Fred would have got one of those discs, though. When I was a recruit, my workaday clothes were a set of dark blue overalls and a cotton excuse for a regular beret; I expect this wasn't much different from what they wore. For live firing or 'musketry instruction,' they went to Williamstown rifle range on the other side of the city. I can still recall the drill instructions, and how big and heavy the 303 was for a slight sixteen-year-old. And the kick it gave and the ringing in my ears of that first shot. I remember, too, the Firing Range Sergeant yelling at me – why was I using my left eye on a right-handed weapon with it on my right shoulder? The 303 was for right-handers, otherwise you got a hot shell casing in your face. Of course, he had no idea I had defective sight in the right eye. It would plague me throughout my military career. Like Fred, I really should not have been recruited in 1958 if the rules had been followed, albeit for a different reason.

Fred's regimental number of 1915, I expect, got him some joshing from his mates. To be given the same number as the year he enlisted seems to me an extraordinary but memorable coincidence; but of course, someone had to get it. I wonder if he saw it as a lucky number. Fate would have it so, as it turned out, if you believe in such things. His medical record on enlistment says he was "five feet four-and-a-half inches, chest thirty-three inches," both measurements below the stated minimum for recruitment at that time. He weighed only one hundred and forty pounds, so he was certainly no strapping farmer. How did Fred cope with what was to come, or even with the training? My record on recruitment shows that we were not that dissimilar physically; there were no such physical constraints for apprentices. So, like me, then, he was no heavyweight or even average at the same age. Like me he would have just peered over the tip of his bayoneted Lee Enfield 303 rifle when standing at attention on parade and given the order 'Right Dress.' How well I remember that first time, wondering when I would be able to look over it!

The use of the bayonet, for which Australian soldiers

would gain some reputation later in Fred's war, was still practised in the Australian Army even in my time, the late 1950s. Bayonet practice took place using hessian bags stuffed with straw, hung on a wooden frame, an ineffective mute substitute for the intended flesh of the enemy. You stand in a line in full battle gear, bayonet attached with rifle muzzle straight out front, stock tight on the hip. When the sergeant yells "charge!" you run full tilt at the bag. You are meant to give a bloodcurdling yell and twist the bayonet as you pull it out – one can guess why. The shouts of "on-guard," ... "in-out-on-guard," would have echoed across the fields of Broadmeadows and raised the lust of those who were yet to know what really to expect. It was, for me, a macabre skill to practise as a teenager. When I remember how I struggled with it, it must have been the same for five-foot-four, one-hundred-and-forty-pound Fred. It would have been rudimentary training at best. The total time in recruit training was around seven weeks, but they weren't yet ready for war; more training was to come in Egypt.

Going on leave was allowed, but only on Sundays, with a pre-embarkation weekend near the end. The accounts include stories by the more local lads of going home on leave as far as Geelong, some thirty-plus miles away. Whether Fred ever got home to St Arnaud for leave before he embarked, we can never know. By the time of his embarkation the 6th was already on Mudros assembled for the assault at Anzac Cove. Whether news about what was going on at the Dardanelles got back to the trainees is not clear from Austin's account of that part of the 6th battalion's war history. I am certain, though, that by Fred's time in training, the word would have got back that they weren't heading for Europe, which might have disappointed him. Halfway through his time at Broadmeadows, on Mar 2 1915, Fred was finally formally enlisted in the 6th and so ready for embarkation to join his unit in Egypt. Around a month later, he would be marching with all his kit from Spencer Street Station to Station Pier to embark on his adventure.

5

EGYPT

Fred embarked from Melbourne for Egypt with the 5th Reinforcement AIF on the HMAT (A20) *Hororata* on April 17, 1915. The *Hororata* was a 9,400 ton ship leased from New Zealand by the Australian Government to form part of "His Majesty's Australian Transport" fleet of ships for troop transport. Although she was a passenger ship, the accommodation for the troops was rudimentary. In fact, the troops slept in hammocks slung over their mess tables, which some commented as "a pretty unsavoury arrangement during rough weather." The image of the ship here in this book shows troops boarding at Melbourne on April 17 1915. So, as Fred's service record shows, he would have been among that orderly mass of troops on the wharf waiting to board. I can imagine them smoking and the banter as they waited to embark. I believe Fred was a smoker all his life, although that's not what killed him in the end. Like those before them, they would stop at Albany on the far southwest coast to await other ships from the east coast forming a convoy.

Fred would not have known then that Western Australia was where his destiny lay. That his life and those of his children to come would all end up not that far north of the grand harbour tucked away at the bottom of the state. It was a place that saw so many pass through who would not return like Fred did, perhaps in a better state than many others. Was it this voyage across the Indian Ocean, via Bombay and the Arabian Gulf and Suez Canal that further fuelled those stories from his family about Malaya? It must have made a huge impression on this sixteen-year-old, travelling alone, in the sense that he was his own man now, one who was considered ready to fight for his country. They disembarked at Suez on May 20 1915, nearly a month after that first Gallipoli landing, a date to be so marked later. They were sent to camp Heliopolis, where Fred would spend the next seven weeks. There, his time was spent in more training that was meant to prepare them for what to expect at Gallipoli.

At Heliopolis, there was more drill, marching, and more trench digging, in desert sand this time. This training was conducted by British Officers and NCOs now, as during this time, all the reinforcements at 'Base,' as it was called, were under the command of the British. This was because the Australian commander at Gallipoli, General Bridges, for his own reasons, divested himself of command of the base operations in Egypt. The war diarist, Bean, relates how that happened, but all of this was way above Fred's concerns. Bean was there in Fred's time and gives an account of this unusual command situation. In effect, there were no Australian command headquarters in Egypt. This situation prevailed until the end of 1915. I believe it was this that accounts for Fred not being repatriated to Australia, though this was what the government wished for convalescing soldiers from the Egypt Expeditionary Force who were unfit for service at the time. It is important to know this in the context of why things happened to him in the way they did.

It was during this period, from when the original battalions arrived, that the British rumoured they considered the AIF to be an ill-disciplined lot. Despite that initial misconception, the 6th, already at Gallipoli under Lt Col George H. Bennett, now promoted to Battalion Commander, became one of the best fighting units in the 2nd Brigade of the AIF. All that would happen very soon, even before they got to France, where they would further excel. But Fred would take no part in any of that later fighting. They had arrived in Egypt well after the main event at Anzac Cove. But the horror stories from the original landing and the Dardanelles campaign generally were all well known amongst the troops. At first, the steady flow of mounting casualties arriving in Egypt caused a rapid build-up in the hospitals there. As Fred left no diary, we cannot know what he was thinking as the information on casualties arrived during the weeks of training at Heliopolis in Egypt. He appears to have left no photographs like those you can find in the archives today, or personal accounts like those of some who were there – some were turned into books. These stories show them on local leave, with photos of them on camels and at the Pyramids. I can only assume he did something like that and gained some local knowledge, as he would claim to speak the local languages later.

It is here that he likely garnered a lot of local detail that he would later apply to describe himself, to create a story much larger than real life about who he was, as he wanted others to see him. It is probably where his fantasies really began. The accounts of the 6th's time at Alexandra and exploits of some of the troops in training and on leave in Cairo are well recorded in Austin's book, and I expect those who followed in the reinforcements mirrored them. It was probably from these early accounts the Battalion got the tag 'rough as bags.' Their reputation as an ill-disciplined lot in Egypt with little respect for authority was probably justified. Disobeying commands, failing to salute, and being absent without leave (AWOL) were the commonest misdemeanours. Some of the service records of Fred's reinforcement group suggest that they followed in the 6th's footsteps. The accounts of absence without leave and disobeying commands seem disproportionate to the numbers involved. Illnesses like pyrexia, diarrhoea, and venereal disease abounded in the service records of many of Fred's cohorts. However, Fred's record for Egypt is a blank on that score. Fred seems to have behaved better than most, as he did not go absent without leave, nor fail to salute whilst there, like so many others. Was it his immaturity that held him back, or just that he didn't get caught?

To give an idea of what he was stepping into and how he got his injury, I revert to the war record. My source is the introductory part of the official Australian War Memorial synopsis on his Battalion's war record at Anzac Cove and

Cape Helles, and its return to the cove, leading up to their participation in the attack on German Officer's Trench; it got that name because a German officer had been seen there at some time. This attack is like a marker for Fred's involvement at Anzac Cove. The 6th took part in the Anzac Cove landing as part of the second wave. Ten days after landing, the 2nd Brigade was transferred south to Cape Helles to help the British in the attack on the village of Krithia. It was at Krithia that the 6th began to get their reputation as an efficient fighting unit. The attack at Krithia captured little ground, but cost the brigade almost a third of its strength – an alarming casualty rate that seemed to be accepted in the unit diaries as the norm for trench warfare at Gallipoli. The 6th alone lost 133 men out of its normal strength of around 700; that's equivalent to losing over a company of men in one action, a shocking statistic. But in the battalion diary which describes the action, it is mentioned in passing.

The 6th returned to Anzac Cove to help defend the beachhead and participate in an action in support of the battle of Lone Pine, a key milestone battle of the campaign. It seems they were spurred on by the high commands urging for more ground to be taken. History shows they did not appreciate the toll it would take on life for no real gain. Lone Pine preparations had commenced by the time Fred had embarked from Alexandria for the Australian front at Gallipoli. His 5th Reinforcement was on its way to what was now the staging post on the Island of Lemnos to prepare for a landing at Gallipoli. After Krithia, the 6th definitely needed reinforcements and it was during the build-up to this battle of Lone Pine that Fred landed with elements of the 5th Reinforcement AIF. He would have been wearing his battalion navy blue over scarlet shoulder patch by now.

6

BLOWN UP AT GALLIPOLI

Fred embarked from Alexandria on the HMT *Scotian* for Mudros on 3 July. Mudros was the Lemnos port, some sixty miles across the sea from the Gallipoli peninsula. It was the staging post for landings at Anzac Cove. According to the recorded campaign history, it was not intended to be so originally – Alexandria was. But as the operations at Gallipoli developed and the carnage and massive re-supply problems began, it soon became the obvious choice. It was not just a staging place for the Australians; all of the allies fighting in the Dardanelles were there, with a number of temporary military hospitals. It had a well-developed harbour with a large local civilian infrastructure. Service records show some fell sick and were hospitalised during this time, and the sicknesses of many weren't just bad luck and the food or hygiene. Yet Fred's military record remained clean for the five days he spent there.

I imagine much of the time was taken up by just sitting around, a common soldiers' plight. His time there, though short, would have included shore landing training. This involved scrambling down nets into the vessels that were to take them ashore, and what to do when on the beach. Whilst this was going on, even though they were some sixty miles away, Fred would have heard the rumble of the

Turkish guns across the water, reminding him of what was to come. During the short time Fred stayed at the dispersal area where they camped, he would have noticed the many arriving wounded and the burials taking place. For the ANZACs after the landing, Mudros had become the next casualty clearing station after Anzac Cove. Preparations for the battles at Lone Pine and German Officer's Trench were now building. The aim was to extend ground already taken at the ANZAC's position, so it was to be a major assault. During this time, heavy shelling by the Turkish using high calibre guns is reported in the 6th war diary – shells about six to eight inches diameter. Fred would definitely have heard this at Mudros; this type of shell would be Fred's nemesis.

I wonder what went through his sixteen-year-old mind when he found himself aboard the ship taking him to land at Anzac Cove. He carried 200 rounds of ammunition with that 303, all he owned, in a pack to be dropped for others to collect once ashore. He was told to write a letter home ready to be sent on death or serious injury, if he was found of course. I suspect Fred did not write to his mother, judging by her written plea for his whereabouts later. His military record states he joined his battalion at Anzac Cove on 10 July. It was recorded after the landing. I have estimated from all the diaries, which included a named officer in the 5th Reinforcement and that he landed sometime during the night of the 9 July, certainly before dawn the next day. The day landings had been discontinued due to the high casualty rates. Bean's account shows why the Turks had made the beach unsafe for daytime landings, although strangely, images survive showing troops playing cricket there some time after the first landings. I found no embarkation list, so could not work out exactly how many troops other than Fred's cohorts of the 5th Reinforcement were in his landing group, but it would have been made up of the remnants of all the units at Anzac Cove's reinforcements waiting at Mudros.

From Bean's and the brigade diary for this period, it seems that many in each reinforcement group fell sick or didn't make it for some other reason. So, it would have been a mixed reinforcement group of well over a hundred who would have landed. There were twenty-three from the 5th Reinforcement that night. Fred doesn't appear to have been assigned to a 6th sub-unit like a company, just to OC Battalion, which means he would be told on landing to follow the man in front to an assembly area near his unit. From seeing the many images in the archives today of what it was like in daylight, it was probably better to arrive at night, regardless of the Turkish artillery. He could not have imagined what it looked like. The first frontline trenches were just over five hundred yards away from the landing place. Shrapnel Gulley was where Fred was heading when he landed, which was the main feature from the beach leading to the front line. When Fred turned up, the 6th was doing one day on/one day off in the front-line trenches, and its HQ was located in the rear area, likely where he ended up after the scramble up the beach, as his record has a cryptic 'reported to unit.' At the same time, the 6th was becoming involved in tunnelling to German Officer's Trench which they were to assault as a supporting action to the main assault on Lone Pine. All of that took place after Fred experienced his first, and, as it turned out, last major attack-related bombardment.

I don't know who Fred's intended Platoon or Company Commander was; the reinforcements were by then never assigned to a specific sub-unit before landing. The battle-hardened soldiers didn't want any fresh-faced newcomer thrust upon them without knowing what they were getting. Reinforcements were eyed off at first to see who was 'good enough.' So, they went to the headquarters or rear area, and a green sixteen-year-old would be easily spotted and left perhaps to linger in support. With reinforcement officers, only older ones were preferred or wanted by some battle-hardened units. Promotion from NCO to officer in the field had become routine by the time Fred got there. With his good record so far, and fertile mind and initiative shown later, if he had been given the chance, Fred might have earned at least a stripe or two, but a Turkish shell or two would intervene. I try to imagine Fred, a slight lad in full battle kit with his pack, rifle at the ready, landing at night on the beach at Anzac Cove, and by dawn of July 10, reaching his unit assembly area. There may have been the noise of random gunfire in his ears and even some shelling, if the Turks had got wind of movement on the beach at night. Although I haven't experienced it in my military life, except on range exercises with live ammunition such as flash-bangs, mortars, tank-gun and 25-pounder, I imagine he must have got the fright of his life and was wondering what he had let himself in for.

What happened to him after that night landing? His medical record has a written notation that tells a different story than what is in the service record, in terms of when he might have arrived and what happened to him. The odds for his group of getting away and surviving without injury can be worked out from what the service record of his contemporaries' injuries show. Of the group of twenty-three who landed that night, in the ensuing days, fourteen were wounded, of which seven were killed in action. So the odds were high that something would happen to him. I know words written about the casualties are old news now, but this became personal because of Fred. From the one hundred and forty of the 5th Reinforcement, and this includes those who went on to France, eighty-four would be wounded, of which twenty would be killed in action. In some killed-in-action cases at Gallipoli, particularly during the high calibre shelling that Fred experienced, if a soldier was not found or remained unidentified, in the court of inquiry that was held to establish the death of a soldier known to have taken part in any action, he was certified as just 'missing in action' – a cold comfort for the family.

Fred's group landed during the 6th's supporting action at German Officer's Trench. That side action turned out to be disastrous for them. During this action, the Turkish high-calibre bombardments in the lead-up and during these operations brought on cases of shellshock, hitherto not encountered at Gallipoli, as Bean records. Fred was there then, but there are those discrepancies in Fred's military service and medical record I needed to resolve. They relate to timing of when things happened to him and what actually happened when he was injured and what the injury was, and when he was evacuated. Both files agree that he was evacuated within the first two weeks of July 1915. Any differences may be reconciled in part by what is contained in the brigade war diaries and Austin's and Bean's description of what the 6th was doing then. Fred's service record states: "Admitted *Gascon* [the hospital ship] [with] Appendicitis." This was not his injury and why he was evacuated, so let's look at the facts.

It is clear that by dawn July 10, Fred was with his battalion, which was near Steele's Post, facing and in the vicinity of German Officer's Trench. The high calibre continuous bombardment of his unit's position began around this time. This is evidenced by the 6th War Diary referring to a large calibre bombardment during early July. This provides the circumstances of him being shelled, although no specific date is mentioned. However, the War Diary of the 7th, which was in the front line for the days 10 and 12 July, records an enemy bombardment using "6 inch howitzers" falling on all the trenches on both those days; on July 13, it says their trenches were almost destroyed. The 6th was in support of the 7th then, and provided them with 100 reinforcements during this period. Fred's medical record states he was 'sent off after being buried by high explosive shell and unconscious for ten hours,' so the injury happened in the period 10 to 13 July; according to his service record he was evacuated to the hospital ship *Gascon* by then. This confirms he was buried by a shell explosion, as it is supported by the diaries and writings of that time; this happened during the operation when the 6th was in support of the 7th in the front-line area during an assault on German Officer's Trench.

Usually the word 'wounded' appeared with an annotation like 'gsw' (gunshot wound), shrapnel etc. Shellshock was not recognised as a 'wound' then. But shellshock was being described at Gallipoli by then, as Bean noted. Around July 13, medical officers, including from the 6th, were describing: "men … in a jumpy condition … wandering around … cases of 'shellshock' were now commonplace." Of course, when Fred reported for his 'Board' review at Harefield in England much later, on July 25 1916, which ultimately led to his discharge unfit for further service, he could have told his own story. I cannot imagine myself, approaching seventeen, going through what he did and not thinking of how to get out of it. However, his 6th service record was written up much later and just followed what was recorded in the medical record and in hospital afterwards. I don't believe he would have made up what happened to him at Anzac Cove, even though he kept it all to himself. It wasn't for appendicitis that he was 'sent off.' There is no doubt in my mind that he was subjected to being shelled and survived, and was not blown to bits like others whose "remains [were] not found." In his record, the appendicitis mentioned developed afterwards. Anyway, it was a serious illness in those days; medicine had made leaps and bounds, but it was still a dangerous operation. As it would transpire for Fred, when his mother found he was on the seriously ill list in the local newspaper.

During my research into the records of Fred's cohorts, particularly for those couple of days at Anzac Cove and for those from his group that lost their lives or were injured, I realised then, more than ever before, that Fred seemed to turn into quite a different person than I had thought he was. My shock is rooted in the deep emotions of loss and futility I felt. The horror of it all, when you read the diaries, was such that I had to take a break at times from reading the various accounts. So many young lives wasted. In his landing cohort of twenty-three, eight were wounded just days afterward in the subsequent ongoing action at German Officer's Trench, and three were killed. Major Peters from his reinforcement was wounded during that shelling and went, with Fred, on the *Gascon* that same day. It's almost as if they were in the exact same spot. Hardest to read about were the death of those whose remains could not be found. Even now, I get that same feeling of shock; it never fails to affect me.

Hospital ships like the *Gascon* would wait off Anzac Cove until they filled up. They usually carried up to four hundred patients, with the seriously wounded placed on deck, as it was a short journey to hospital help. This was because, at the beginning of the Dardanelles campaign, the original intention was to take casualties direct to Malta or

Alexandria. But, before Fred's time and after the ANZAC landing, because of the high volume of casualties, the practice had been to go directly to Mudros on the island of Lemnos and offload the urgent cases, then proceed to Malta with the rest. The high casualty rate was why there was a build-up of temporary hospitals on Mudros by the participating armies, British as well as Australian and New Zealand. There are plenty of well-written, moving accounts from Australian nurses serving on Mudros that describe this situation. So, Fred returned to Mudros but did not get off-loaded, and that sealed his future. If he had been considered seriously wounded he would have most likely ended up back in Australia. If he had been off-loaded at Mudros, he would have ended up in the No.1 Auxiliary Australian Hospital and in the care of his own people, but fate intervened. His was not an urgent case as he had no visible wound, so he was taken to Malta and Tigné Hospital run by the British. It was once a military barracks for the Royal Garrison Artillery; they had vacated it and it was prepared as a hospital in June 1915. Tigné was for the minor wounded. There weren't any Australian doctors at Tigné and no Australian administrative command at that time in Malta. So, his chances of getting back to Australia from Malta as "unfit for further service" ended there.

His medical record says he arrived in Malta on 18 July and his appendicitis must have developed some time from then, as he appeared in his record as dangerously ill on July21. Annie had sent a telegram to the Secretary of

Defence, Army, stating her address as the Waterloo plains farm on July 20, asking for her son's whereabouts. She had a reply on 21 July from the army stating with regret he was dangerously ill and she would be advised "full particulars." He remained on the dangerously ill list until August 6 and appeared in the sixty-first casualty list in all the main Australian daily newspapers on August 7 1915, and this was no doubt read by his mother. So, Fred, it seems, had not been writing home. The day after the official list was published in early August, Annie sent another letter to the Melbourne Army Headquarters with a letter enclosed for Fred and a returned stamp envelope for him. In that letter, she said she had written to him regularly, but he never replied. She got a number of further army telegrams, one with an address of the hospital in Malta, the last telling her he had been sent to England, with an address to write to in both cases.

Remember, she had his twin not yet seventeen by her side when he left to go to war. So it was a seminal moment for me when I read her words asking about her son, I imagined her relief that he had survived so far. Knowing he had enlisted and with probably no letters from him her eye would have surely been on the regular casualty lists appearing in the papers, with the accounts of what was happening at Gallipoli. Although it would appear from Annie's later letters that he never wrote to her, he would not forget her entirely. I found a record that he had at some time allotted four shillings a day from his pay to her. This would remain effective until May 5 1916, when he was discharged, even though he had found a wife before that.

Why was Fred sent to England and not Australia to recuperate, when he was apparently still not fit for duty, even if he had recovered from his appendix operation? It was because he was in a British hospital and just lumped in with all the others. The answer also lay in the lack of an Australian Headquarters in Egypt, even well after the Dardanelles campaign had started. There was no Australian voice in that rear echelon able to make a decision as to where to send casualties like Fred. It is on record that the Australian Government wanted recovering wounded sent home, but for many that just did not happen. For that, one could blame General Bridges, based on what Bean said about it all; but, as Bridges died of his wounds at Gallipoli, it is perhaps unfair to put it on one person's shoulders. Soon afterwards, his replacement, General Birdwood, did institute an Australian rear echelon command structure in Egypt that took such decisions away from the British. If he had gone to an Australian hospital there, it is likely he would have been medical-boarded for a "change" as they called it, and sent home. But no, it was to England he went and not alone; Major Peters was at Tigné with that gunshot wound to the shoulder, obviously seen also as minor. Peters would end up in England after travelling on the same vessel as Fred, then go to France, but not with the 6th, get wounded again, and return home in 1916. I would think, judging by what followed, Fred was quite happy that he ended up in London and not back in Australia.

Fred embarked with Major Peters on August 18 on the HMT *Asturias,* another passenger liner that had been converted to a hospital ship, and arrived at Bethnal Green Hospital London on August 26 1915. My siblings and I travelled on the same-named ship to Australia. So we, and later, Daphne, left England on the replacement ship some thirty years on. What were the odds of that occurring, I wondered? Fred's *Asturias* would be torpedoed near the end of his war; ours carried many more migrants like us. And I wondered about that Major Peters; could he have taken Fred under his wing at this time? They must have crossed paths a number of times up until they landed together at Anzac Cove. Remember, Peters commanded Fred's reinforcement group. I wondered if he could have filled the role of a father figure for Fred. Peters was in his forties and married; I do not know whether he had children. However, I tend to think Fred didn't need a father by then. Did Fred talk to Peters at all to learn about his background – how he became an officer, perhaps? Peters had gained his commission through the University Officer Training Corps. Did Fred begin to think of re-inventing himself as the audacious and bogus Captain Bibby, DSC, from what he might have learned on the *Asturias*?

Fred's Beazleys Bridge School and vegetable garden, 1907.
(Private collection)

Fred, on the right, with his mother and brothers at Everton Farm, St Arnaud, around 1912. Older brother William Raub seated.
(Private collection)

Army Apprentices' Senior Class Coral Sea Battle march in Melbourne, May 1960. Somewhere in there is me with 303 and bayonet fixed, similar to what Fred was issued. (Private collection)

HMT *Hororata* embarking 5th Reinforcement, Melbourne, April 1915. (Courtesy AWM archive)

HMT *Scotian Alexandria*, the vessel that took Fred to Mudros in preparation for the landing at Anzac Cove, 1915. (Courtesy AWM archive)

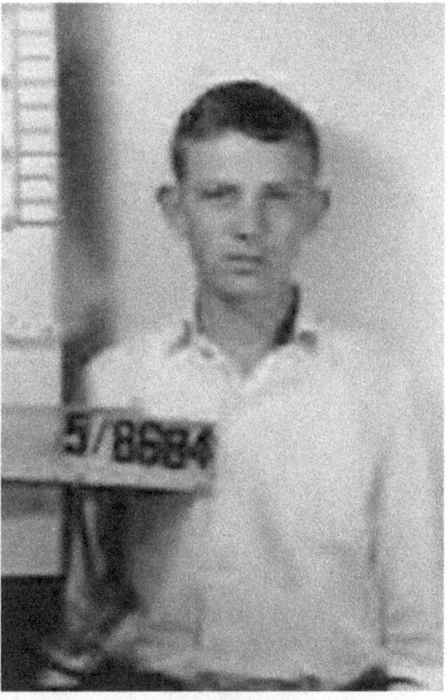

Left: Landing boat loading practice, Mudros, 1915. Right: Me, signing up as a 16 year old Army Apprentice, Fremantle, January 1958. Same enlistment month, age, height and build as Fred when he signed up in 1915. Fred boarded such a boat 5 months after his enlistment, bound for Anzac Cove. (image of Mudros courtesy AWM archive)

Hospital ship HMMS *Gascon* that took Fred to Malta, 1915. (Courtesy AWM archive)

Tigne Military Hospital with tents for overflow patients, Malta, 1915. (Courtesy www.militaryhospitalsmalta)

SS *Asturias*, hospital ship that took Fred to England, 1915.
(Courtesy AWM archive)

Bethnal Green Military Hospital, East End, London, 1916.
(Private collection)

15 Sprowston Road, Forest Gate on left, 2011. (Private collection)

York House furnished apartments today. (Private collection)

Lowestoft Esplanade showing Victoria Road. York House left of picture on the facing corner, 1950s. (Courtesy Lowestoft Heritage Workshop)

HH the Maharaja Sir Sri Krishna raja Bahadur, GCSI, GBE, ruler of Mysore in 1920. It was his brother-in-law Fred met with in London to obtain the position in Mysore. (Courtesy V&A collection)

British Indian Passport, 1933. (Courtesy V&A collection)

Imperial Hotel, Russell Square, 1942. (Private collection)

Fred, at right, with his twin Arthur, at left and William, centre. Melbourne, early 1920s. (Private collection)

Fred at right with unknown others, at a wedding at St Marys Bromley, Kent, mid-1940s. Probably not long before he went to sea on the SS *Moreton Bay*. (Fred's collection)

SS *Moreton Bay* of P&O Line, 1922. She was sold to the Commonwealth Line which serviced Australia regularly. Fred served onboard as a Steward from 1949 until 1952. (Private collection)

7

FRED AND GRACE

From the end of August 1915 and during his time at Bethnal Green Hospital, the activity recorded in Fred's medical files gives a hint of what his intention now was regarding his military career, and Australia, for that matter. I believe that he deliberately put his family and Australia at the back of his mind. London was a far cry from country Victoria. He had decided this was where he wanted to stay. It was a time when, I am certain, he had a lot to think about, and he made up his mind he wasn't going back to the front in Egypt or France, or to St Arnaud, for that matter. Was this when he began to realise that he needed to create another self, after enlisting so young and with no qualifications other than completing high school? He probably saw that he was as qualified in life experience as many of his compatriots, if not more so – he had been born in Malaya and had gone to war. As for the military, he would have seen many men with physical wounds, and he appeared, on the face of it, unwounded. But here he was, evacuated as wounded to England with this new 'wound' called shellshock. How would that look in St Arnaud if he returned? What he did next certainly shows that he did not wish to go back to Australia. There was no comparison between Australia and St Arnaud and London, even in wartime, and no doubt he saw more opportunities there than farming.

From this period on, it became clear that he persisted with the fiction that he was older than he was – but why? In Malta, he'd turned seventeen, still too young to serve, by Australian standards. If he revealed his real age, how could he prove it? I am certain he didn't have a birth certificate. His birth date could have been confirmed in some way, say by his mother; she knew where he was by this time. She had been in contact with the military a number of times, and surely her intervention would have made them send him home to Australia. However, I found no other record of such a case, and it seems unlikely at this stage that it would have made any difference. As the records for others show, he was not alone; what about Lowe, also from St Arnaud, who was the same age and who went on to France? There were others like him, such as sixteen-year-old Joseph Byers, who lied about his age to enlist in the British Army and was the first to be executed for running away from the shelling early in 1915. That showed there was little sympathy in the military in England for people Fred's real age at the Front. Whereas the Australians refused to execute deserters and he may have known about that. There was some underlying reason why Fred would not reveal his true age, and did not reveal his actual whereabouts in England to his family at home.

After arrival in August 1916, his service record shows a quiet period. There is nothing in his military or medical record as to what happened in Bethnal Green hospital from when he arrived until around the first week of October. I assume he was deemed recovered to some degree, as he would soon be discharged from there. But before that he had some furlough from hospital, and he met a woman who became his first wife. I could find no Bethnal Hospital patient record, so I cannot know what his official or true state was at that time. Although he must have been still their patient, and he definitely wasn't deemed ready, officially that is, to go back to war. Although Annie knew where he was, he was not writing home. But the information on what he was doing and his whereabouts came from another source, an Australian local newspaper. From this news, it became clear what he was up to while at Bethnal. What he did during his time there was pretty dramatic for a seventeen-year-old; little did he know some of it would become public back home so soon. He took furlough to stay at an address in Forest Gate in east London on the Romford Road, and this was where he found a new home for a while. The local newspaper report was in his home paper, the *St Arnaud Mercury* on December 8 1915, and told a story of a 'brave little fellow, whose bright cheerful ways would be missed when he left ...' This was an extract from a letter sent by a Mrs L.A. Lambert from England around October 1915. So begins the story of how Fred met his first Grace (there would be another Grace in Australia), and how Annie came to find out what Fred was up to in London. It has some of the ingredients of a romantic wartime novel, which is probably why it got the attention in St Arnaud it did, with a rather dramatic, if misleading heading: "LETTERS FROM THE FRONT – PRIVATE F. BIBBY."

Mrs Lambert's letter was sent to her cousin in Melbourne, a Mrs Storer of St Kilda. She wrote asking if her cousin knew anybody who could help trace the relatives of Fred, who was 'wounded at Gallipoli' and had been staying with her at her home. There were many of Fred's relatives in Victoria. He had three uncles, all with family there at that time. It turned out Mrs Storer knew of a person named Bibby working in a bank in Albury, on the border of Victoria and New South Wales. This was William Raub, Fred's older brother, who was starting a career with the Union Bank, later to become the Australian & New Zealand bank. William would enlist in 1916 and serve in the Ambulance Corps in Egypt, and return to work for the same bank for the rest of his life. That is how that letter got to Annie via her eldest son. But why did it have to happen this way, why didn't Fred just write home to say what he was about? The Lamberts obviously knew he was an Australian soldier, but for some reason, he was keeping quiet about the details of his Australian origins. The letter said that he had been staying on furlough for two weeks with Mrs Lambert at 15 Sprowston Road, Forest Gate, most likely in the first two weeks of October 1915. Mrs Lambert had three daughters, the youngest already married, and the eldest was Grace Constance, who was in her early thirties and still living with her. Grace was on her way to being a spinster; with a war on, eligible bachelors would have been in short supply, so the arrival of a young Australian soldier was likely very welcome in the Lambert household.

The description of Fred in this letter suggests that she

saw him as perhaps not quite eligible in terms of maturity or stature. She stated he had been staying at her home a fortnight and his furlough had been extended for another 14 days. He was doing well, but was not medically fit to go back to the front, as he could not bear the heavy weight the soldiers had to carry. He had done his share and his relatives would be proud of him. Then follows the brave little fellow bit. She also said that, at the conclusion of his furlough, he was expected to be sent to the front again, and that he was not strong by any means and that he had had two operations besides concussion of the brain. Operations, concussion of the brain! Are those Fred's inventions and words or something he heard in hospital? There is nothing in his medical record about operations in this period. The letter suggests that Fred spent most of October out of hospital at Forest Gate with Grace and her mum.

Perhaps Mrs Lambert was on some official list as a place to stay for soldiers. She called her place Iddesliegh, after the Devonshire village. The house still exists and looks just like an upmarket semi of the period. It seems Fred, by the end of October 1915, had found a new home in England and a girlfriend much older than himself. On documents that follow, he would state he was in his twenties, even though still only seventeen. Grace clearly accepted him for what he said he was – a mature twenty-year-old. As far as operations at Bethnal, there are none in his medical record. His diagnosis was 'Debility and Pneumonia'. Fred was right, though, about going back to the Front; the military wheels were turning for him to return to duty. He was on a list to be eventually sent to a place in Dorset where many Australians were after recovery pending assignment to Egypt or France. It depended upon where their unit was at the time. By this time the 6th was in France and at the front and regularly under fire, commanded by Lt Col Bennett, their Gallipoli commander.

I can readily picture Fred in my mind from that time. He would have been issued with new uniform, and it was likely all he wore at that time. I see him on furlough wearing his slouch hat, giving him some extra height. He had not grown much, from Mrs Lambert's account, and wouldn't, judging by later photos. My recollections of him later in life are that he was no taller than me, if not shorter; he may have added an inch or so to his five-foot-four-plus on enlistment. He must have cut a slight figure still, but his demeanour and what he thought about himself was something else. He had been to Egypt and Gallipoli, seen the Suez Canal and Colombo, and been born in the 'exotic' East. He might have begun to see himself as something other than just a farm boy from St Arnaud by this time. He must have been very observant and had accumulated a smattering of knowledge of those places, which he would use to good effect soon. He was also very resourceful, perhaps to offset his diminutive physical presence.

He seemed to want to build a new life for himself, and he persisted in saying he was much older than he was, and more qualified. By November 1915, Fred was back from his

Bethnal furlough and was sent to Leighton VAD Hospital in Bedfordshire after he had in effect created a 'new' Fred at Forest Gate, London in October. Whether yet fit for service is not clear as the record doesn't say that, or explain in the record why he was sent to another hospital. This was Leighton VAD (Voluntary Aid Detachment) Hospital, Leighton (Leighton Buzzard) in Bedfordshire, just over forty-five miles from north London. Such places had no medical staff, only nursing aides; they were places for rehabilitation. He would stay there until December19. It was not uncommon to send Australian casualties in England to distant hospitals like VADs for final recuperation. It was here that he would get the first blemish in his service record.

From his service record, his military behaviour so far, compared with of some of his cohorts, appears to have been exemplary. There had been no going absent without leave (AWOL), or worse, such as disobeying commands, and other exploits, either at base or on training in Egypt or at Mudros. Any of the same behaviour would have been recorded during this early period in London and other nearby places. So he must have been attached to some Australian military unit, because after arriving at Leighton he went AWOL for the first time, according to his service record. Even in my time, this was tantamount to desertion of duty, and was punished severely – more so, I expect, in war time. The record states he went AWOL from November 19 for four days, for which he got docked four days' pay and ninety-six hours detention. Detention just meant he could not leave the premises, as Leighton was just a hospital, not a barracks with guards at the gate. This is the first recorded blot on his conduct since he enlisted.

It is clear it was to visit Grace, as this relationship continued. At this stage it was pretty clear that Fred was not the deserting type, as he returned to Leighton. His record of service states he was discharged from there on 19 December to join the 'Australian Military Offices,' which may have been what was called a holding unit, on paper only, until his future was sorted out. It looked after soldiers that did not have a unit and the army didn't yet know what to with. He was sent on furlough, to be spent with Grace no doubt, until the end of January 1916. Problems with his eyes are recorded in the medical record, but nothing is mentioned about what was done about it. He is then shown to be on strength at a camp called the Australian Intermediate Depot in Abbey Wood, in Southeast London near Greenwich, south of the Thames. This was a military camp set up for what I can only assume were itinerant Australian troops such as Fred. Even after this considerable period of Bethnal hospitalisation and Leighton rehab, his medical record did not yet say 'fit for service.'

The decision on what to do with Fred seemed to be a very prolonged one, as he seemed to be passed from 'pillar to post.' From all reports, Abbey Camp was a well-disciplined place, with the Provost Corps (Military Police) in control. As well as those 'in transit' it held 'prisoners' like soldiers in detention, including deserters. The reports on the place show that there were many going AWOL. I do not know if he was one of those in the beginning, but he soon put himself on that list. He was at Abbey Wood for six weeks, but on March 22, he again went AWOL. I have no doubt that this was to visit Grace. It was for five days, for which he got 120 hours detention, and he was docked for five days' pay. After he had done his 'time' he was placed on the Nominal Roll of the Egypt Expeditionary Force 27th Draft; this meant he was destined for France if he was to rejoin the 6th, but the record doesn't mention his assigned service Unit. Some troops like him did go back to Egypt, where the AIF Expeditionary Headquarters were still, rather than join their original unit. It appeared that he was headed back to the front by the end of March 1916, be it France or Egypt. But he still had to pass a medical board before that could happen, and it seems Fred had other ideas about his future.

What about Grace Lambert at Forest Gate? How did she fare, with Fred appearing on furlough from various places, on leave and going AWOL? Their marriage took place on February 28 1916, so one weekend, on leave from Abbey Wood he got married to Grace Lambert, a spinster aged thirty-three, at the Romford Road Congregational Church at Forest Gate. He stated he was twenty-one, a bugler in the AIF, and a railway clerk. If he was a bugler, there is not a hint of this in his record. Army musicians ended up as stretcher bearers, and he wasn't one of those at Gallipoli. The witnesses were Grace's mother and a Julia Garrard. Both fathers are shown as deceased. Clearly, the reason he went AWOL in March from Abbey Wood was to visit his new wife. He was not yet eighteen. The letter from Mrs Lambert suggests that the seeds were sown for this marriage back in October 1915.

Grace, a woman almost twice his age, may have been a mother figure to replace Annie. He was still very young, and may also have seen some sort of financial security in the union. Her age must have been obvious, but her family was well established. The Lamberts were apparently middle class, which would have been important for him, considering the home he came from. Obviously, her mother approved, glad to see her eldest married off at last. Fred left no photographs from this period in his life, so I cannot picture them together. They might have made an odd couple, given the age difference and Fred's stature and appearance. They weren't yet living as man and wife, as he was still in the army and a war was on. After marking time at the Abbey Wood camp, at the beginning of June 1916, he was sent to No.1 Australian Auxiliary Hospital, Harefield, which was just northwest of London. No reason is given, but he must have exhibited some signs of 'the mind illness' while at Abbey Wood camp. He was discharged from the Harefield hospital at the end of June. There he had been 'boarded' as permanently unfit for service in the AIF at home or abroad. He was then sent to the Commonwealth Depot in Weymouth on the Dorset coast for processing. The Weymouth camp at that time was crowded with recuperated Australian troops waiting to return to service. I found many stories written about the Australians' time there. The street names that remain today reflect the Australian presence from that time.

As he had been declared unfit for further service, sending him to Dorset was just for administrative reasons, as there was no suggestion that he was headed back to the front. Fred was discharged on August 11 1916 in London. His board' record on 25 June 1916 states: *'complains of giddiness and headaches. No objective signs of disease. Neurasthenia renders him permanently unfit ... Service has aggravated the pre-existing condition ... 6 years ago had a nervous breakdown, was under treatment and at rest for 6 months.'* Clearly a tale he told, as six years earlier, he was eleven.

I wish I had an image of him then. Fred's medical report on an invalid army form B179 of July 27, 1916 was the instrument of his discharge from the AIF in England. He was discharged due to *'Shellshock.'* On his discharge documents he said he was twenty-three, and his occupation was 'Author,' both seemingly accepted by the army as true. And so, the new persona began to emerge. He did not request repatriation, perhaps because of his married state. There is no record that he told the army of his marital status. But he clearly did not wish to go home; London was his home now. I can only assume that after his discharge he was living with Grace and her mother and continued to do so, at least for the time being. There is no military record about Grace other than the pay allotment, which shows the army knew he had another dependent; but did he actually declare he was married to a British national? He now appeared to be settling down in England. But this marriage would remain a secret from his immediate family, and I do not know whether he ever told them.

So, Fred's brief military career ended with his discharge in England after his unlikely marriage to a much older woman. The description of what happened at Gallipoli was my way to better understand what happened afterward. With no personal anecdotes from Fred or from any personal diary or other accounts than the sparse and confusing military records, it was a puzzle to put the picture together. There are inconsistencies in his record I could not ignore. Nowhere in his service record does it mention him being 'unconscious for ten hours.' It is only in his medical record, which was compiled separately, and later. His statement to the medical Board that his former trade or occupation as an 'author' might suggest he believed he was. Just as he said he was a train driver – both something better than what he really was. But, an author – did he have an idea of writing about his awful experience? He could write a convincing letter, as we will see, and certainly was resourceful, and had ideas to become something better in life than a farmer. He was now approaching eighteen, just on the verge of manhood. He might have seen 'author' as a smart thing to say, despite his obvious lack of formal education beyond high school.

There was no need to make a story up to impress the military authorities, or anybody else later, into believing what happened to him on July 13 1915, near German Officer's Trench; that was true life. He was there and was shelled and buried for some time, unconscious; this is supported by the military record of events. There is no doubt that Fred's experience at Anzac Cove changed his life forever. One could say he was broken in some way from then on; we now know that shellshock is a real injury. He probably never really came to terms with the fact he was discharged without visible signs of injury after only a short time at war. He might have seen it as a stigma on his character and carried that with him all his life. At that time, shellshock was not yet seen by many as a real injury. Nor was there was such a diagnosis as post-traumatic stress disorder then, or any treatment for it. He was a damaged man at this point in his life.

8

CAPTAIN BIBBY I PRESUME

During the period he was hospitalised, though Fred didn't write home to Annie at Waterloo Plains, the army did. They wrote first in September 1915, telling her he was on the hospital ship *Asturias* heading for England, and again, the same month, that he was in hospital in London with the Bethnal address. I cannot imagine she didn't write back to him then, knowing where he was. Then again, in April 1916 the army wrote that he had returned to Egypt in March. At that time, Fred was in Abbey Wood waiting for his medical board. This information was retracted by another letter to Annie shortly after, saying he had been discharged in London. It seems, for the military, there was a time when the left hand didn't know what the right was doing, which might have worked in Fred's favour. It was unlikely she knew what had happened to him in between the first army letter saying he was heading for England from Malta and the last saying he was discharged in London. I don't think she knew he had married Grace Constance Lambert of Forest Gate. Fred had started a new life in England and wasn't coming home. Well, not yet, anyway. So, what really happened to him from now on?

Fred's some nineteen months service in the AIF had ended with the issue of his certificate of discharge, which was sent to the Forest Gate address. I would serve for twenty-one years and never go to war so I never faced the perils he had in his short career. The discharge certificate says his character was 'very good.' He was said to be five foot six, twenty-two, and his trade was 'clerk,' not bugler anymore. Again, a new occupation and his age older than he was, but now officially recognised – as good as a birth certificate, which clearly, he did not have. But this was an important document for him, which could be used as his modus operandi, as it's unlikely he would have been able to obtain a birth certificate from Australia, nor would he want one. It also stated he was permanently unfit for service at home or abroad, which would protect him from what was to come – another world war. With the certificate came a release document for him to sign. It is interesting; in another piece of misinformation, it states he was in the Australian Light Horse. The other important information is that he signed away, except for any military war pension or gratuity, any other entitlements, including repatriation to Australia. I find it hard to understand why he did that, but he probably had no choice if he chose to be discharged in England. He had a wife in London, and the army would not have repatriated her; moreover, she still did not appear in his service record, which said his marital status was single. So, Fred, with the help of the army, had quite successfully re-invented himself, as a mature age, adult clerk, yet he was only eighteen, with no qualifications. He might have felt the world was his oyster.

He had spent most of his 'military career' in and around London and its near counties. It was time spent learning to know his adopted country and prepare for the next period of his life. He had a lot of time on furlough, more than in hospital. He had seen parts of the country from Dorset to Bedfordshire and outer London. That it took well over twelve months to find himself a civilian in England is due to the administration of his case by the Australian military system, then operating in London. It was an inordinate amount of time, and I wonder how much of that was down to Fred and his desire to avoid going back to the Front. He must have learned a lot from it, judging by his next step. He had become a good storyteller. Maybe that 'author' tag in his medical board papers meant something after all. Was this j the real Fred emerging?

On April 17 1917, he got his 'King's Certificate on Discharge,' which had been posted to him at Forest Gate. This was a ceremonial certificate for "Men who served the Empire" given only to all Commonwealth 'other ranks,' that is, not officers, who were discharged through wounds or disabilities. It was an important document and something I would have expected him to want to keep. It took so long to arrive after his discharge because it was a new award, gazetted in England first in 1917, even later in Australia. He returned the signed receipt the next day from the same address. So, he was still in London a year after discharge and had well and truly burned his boats with the military, as well as his family in Australia, by the looks of it. But what was he doing during the eight months or so in London before that certificate arrived, and where were Grace and her mother? I don't think he just twiddled his thumbs; he had a grand plan afoot. The lad from St Arnaud, ex-private of the 6th, had decided to become an officer and a gentleman.

What about this family in England? He had an aunt with a big family not far away. Did his mother write to him at some time about his Aunt Nellie? His mother was with Nellie when they were at Raub; so they were likely close. Nellie would have known Fred's father and him as a baby. Nellie lived close to London during this time. This was Fred's deceased father's younger sister living with her husband and their children at Heston Hall in Heston Middlesex, not that far away. The information could have come to him by letter from his mother when she knew where he was, and surely, he got some from her, forwarded by the army. I cannot imagine the military not making sure they were sent on to his various hospitals, and camps like Abbey Wood and Weymouth.

Nellie, or Phyllis Evelyn Helen, the youngest daughter of William, had married an ex-India army captain in Bombay in 1899. She had three daughters and a son by this time. They had lived in Bombay for a short while before the war, but were back in England by the start of Fred's war, and would remain there. Nellie's husband, Cecil, was at this time serving in France. After the war, and during the events that follow that involved Fred, Cecil would become a Lt Col RAMC. Cecil had 'good connections'; one of his daughters would marry a Lord of the Realm and another, a WWII

General. They lived in a house with servants, fertile ground for Fred's idea of the type of people he wanted to be with. This was Fred's close family and could potentially be fuel for his imagination. Could he have visited them and learned more about the Orient to add to his brief sojourn passing through the ports of Bombay, Aden, and in Alexandria – information he would use in his new persona?

When the army sent me to England in 1969, Nellie, in her 90s, was living in Norfolk, but I did not know that, and had no one to tell me otherwise, unlike Fred. I had a photo of Nellie's father then; it would stay with me over the years and spawn that book, *William's Story*. It would be many years before I knew about Nellie and Fred's life in England, and what happened to him there. I didn't know that Norfolk would be Fred's stamping ground, either.

Soon after the war, Grace and her mother moved to York House, Lowestoft. Records show Fred there also, but he did not stay; he could not have, from what later transpired. Fred had more to do in London, and returned there. Lowestoft was certainly a step up for Fred. York House in Lowestoft was south of the river estuary and in a better part of town. It was where people went to promenade, not bathe in the sea; no public bathing took place near the adjacent Claremont Pier. Then, it was a growing town with a population that had increased a hundredfold by the 1900s. It was popular with some of the wealthy families who had villas there, where they holidayed. Assuming Fred had no qualifications and was recently discharged, how could

Grace's mother afford to live in furnished apartments in a salubrious part of a fashionable seaside town? Was it the sale of 15 Sprowston Road in Forest Gate? Yet, later there is a suggestion it was still in the family.

Before spending any time in Lowestoft, I'm sure Fred stayed at Forest Gate and took the opportunity to explore the West End of London. So, was Fred earning now? I think more likely he might have been living off the Lamberts. I don't think the money to fund what he did came from Australia. I had hoped there would have been some record of his travel to Australia and back to visit his family during this early period. Australian soldiers were much higher paid than the British, but it is hard to think he might have saved up much from his five shillings a day pay when he was serving, particularly with a wife to support. And he had left himself only a shilling day before he married Grace; the rest had gone to his mother. Although it appears out of character so far for him to think of his family, he would have had good reason to go to Melbourne now. His mother had moved there from St Arnaud. His brothers were also there, one still with the Bank and the other becoming a pharmacist.

He wasn't entirely finished with the army, despite not bothering to pick up his service medals from Australia House. He still had a war gratuity to collect and would return to Australia for that, but later. If he did return at this time, it might have been under an alias. Maybe he did go home and just left no trace; he could have signed on as crew.

This post-war period had the usual cast of lost souls looking for the next adventure, like Fred. His mother had sold that land in St Arnaud, so maybe! It appears that he had funds, but they could not have been from his army days. As far as I could work out, they came from his mother-in-law, and from his mother, if you believe what the press claimed later.

He was preparing himself for a new persona. In early 1920, we come to the beginning of a fascinating sequence of events. It may not be as significant as some of the similar stories of the time, but taking into account where he came from, to me, it was a 'grand deception.' Like an earlier Walter Mitty, Fred's new persona began from the start of his civilian life in London. Judging by the breadth of his scheme, he must have been working very early to create this new self. I believe not even Grace was privy to what he planned. The first notice of this is a letter he wrote on August 24 1920 to the Secretary, Political Department of the India Office, with a completed application form, asking to be appointed a commission in the Indian Army. I can only imagine that he became aware that a position was available for a qualified person in the Indian State of Mysore from newspaper reports or advertisements. It is unlikely he had established connections with people who moved in the circles of the India Office, or got to know anybody who had lived and worked there. However, his Aunt Nellie and her husband Cecil's strong links to India from service in the Indian Army spring to mind. Cecil may have known most of the main characters in the India Office whose attention

Fred would attract.

Fred obviously used the military knowledge he had acquired to date to invent a Captain Bibby, with a DSC, no less. He would also call himself a Dr Bibby, Mr. Bibby, Barrister-at-law, and Mr. Bibby M.Sc. He might have used, or planned to use, all of these persona at some time in the years up to 1920 and later, if he had been successful. Trying to imagine him then, I look at the photo of him with his brothers, which I think was taken near this time in Melbourne; he looks so out of place. It looks as if he just dropped in for the session. He looks dapper in a lounge suit and waistcoat and crisp white shirt with a Windsor knotted tie. His brothers are in dinner dress of sorts. It shows he was up with the fashion in London of the time. He looks like a Dr Bibby to me. I believe that this photograph was taken after this episode, that is, after he had been discovered. He looks like a man about town, London, not Melbourne!

Fred's letter to the India Office is audacious; I found it astonishing that he thought all he stated would be accepted as true without a shred of written evidence provided. It is breathtaking in its bravado for someone of his age. I wonder whether to class him as a rogue, or just a dreamer. He had just turned twenty-two, so where did this idea come from? It does show Fred had an enormous amount of self-belief then. Also, that he had learned a lot about the military and how to become an officer, amongst other things. It is addressed from York House, Victoria Road, Lowestoft. The handwriting is clear, with a confident signature, and it is well written, considering he only went to high school. He portrays himself as a man of the world, and much older in experience than he was in years. The style is as if he has already had a meeting with the recipient and is following advice given, suggesting he has already got his foot in the door. It suggests maybe somebody in the India Office might have been aware of his intent. He wrote:

> As requested I herewith enclose form for temporary employment in the Indian Army duly filled in. I note the enclosed form relating to terms of service that "No candidate can be accepted who has not served with an Indian unit for at least one year." I regret to say I am not able to fulfil that clause but I have had a number of years in the East since childhood, and have a good knowledge of the following countries India, Persia, Mesopotamia and Egypt, for the last ten years my business has been connected with the natives of the above countries. I not only know the natives well, but I have a thorough knowledge of the countries mentioned. I have had experience in obtaining native labour and controlling same. My army experience is not very extensive, although I have had about six years army experience. First in the University O.T.C. then as a Lieut. in the Australian Military Service, and two years active service during the war in the Dardanelles, Egypt and Canal. I beg leave to point out that I contemplate sailing from London about the middle of September for Bangour [He means Bangor and this is underlined in blue pencil by the India Office] and unless I hear anything further from you, I shall conclude my application does not fulfil your conditions of service I may add I have a slight knowledge of languages in the countries mentioned.

Apart from the obvious untruths, the enclosed form is full of claims which were false. That he was educated at Scotch College, a prestigious Australian Private School, completed second year law at Melbourne University, but failed to continue. That he was presently a merchant, buying and selling in Bangalore, India and Egypt. That he had lived in the East since childhood for fourteen years and had a thorough knowledge of "Natives" in the countries he names. And to boot, a "fair knowledge" of all the languages of the countries mentioned. Interestingly, he gave his mother-in-law's house address in Forest Gate as his permanent address. How to explain these brazen claims?

I see him completely consumed by the sophistication of it. I see him looking at all the people around him, the way they dressed and spoke, particularly in the West End. I think he said to himself that was what he wanted to be part of. All fuelled by family stories in his youth. The stories of his grandfather who began as a toolmaker and became quite a man of importance in Singapore, for example, and who had a poem and eulogies published about him in *The Straits Times* when he died. Why did he need to become an officer in the Indian army; he only needed a particular passport? Passport visas for India didn't exist then, so firstly he needed to become an officer of the Political Department of the India Office. That letter from him is the opening document of an extraordinary India Office case file in the British Library in London all about Fred. In essence, the file is about the issue of a special passport and the lengths he went to obtain it. It begins in the middle of 1920 and ends with a court case in November that year.

He took up residence in a hotel in the West End; this must have been before August 1920, from the events that followed. These events took place over a period of some weeks and involved timing his presence with the visit of certain people to London. A certain entourage from India was expected in town and became the focus of his attention. This Indian royal visit can be narrowed down to an article in the *Pall Mall Gazette* of August 11 1920, announcing the arrival of a Crown Princess from Mysore at Deauville France; they were on their way to London. Did Fred ingratiate himself with an Indian gentleman who was part of that entourage? Sindar Lakshmi Kandaraj Urs was the brother-in-law of the Maharajah of Mysore. This gentleman was also the Prime Minister (Diwan) of Mysore. Perhaps he was arranging more Rolls Royce cars for his Maharaja, one of the richest men in the world. Urs was also looking for a secretary and manager for the Maharaja. Fred was convincing enough, apparently, to obtain this position under the guise of a Captain Bibby residing at The Imperial Hotel, Russell Square.

The file indicates he actually got the job! How many applied for this position is lost to history. How did Fred, who by all accounts had a less than commanding physical presence, come to know the gentleman and gain his trust to obtain such a position? Fred became almost a likeable person to me after this revelation. He had well and truly acquired the 'gift of the gab.' He must have had a wardrobe as well, to go with this new persona. When staying in London in the East End many years later, long after the original Imperial had been replaced, I bought a couple of bespoke suits from a Mayfair tailor. The suit he is wearing in that photo of the brothers might have come from a similar establishment.

Again, where did the money come from to pay the hotel bill and support this lifestyle he clearly had adopted?

What he needed was a British India Passport as part of the plan for working in India; in those days one couldn't reside there without one. There is a 'Miss Parr' mentioned in the file; her role was to be his 'wife,' for the position required that he have one. She was also to be a companion to the daughter of the Maharaja in Mysore. I wonder what special qualifications Miss Parr had, other than being single and eligible, according to Fred. The later press record indicated she was a local Norwich lady, but little else is revealed, and my search for her was futile. He had a wife already, but clearly he felt Grace, at thirty-three plus, was not up to the position. What's more, she knew who he really was. He clearly planned to leave her behind. The letters from the Norwich police in the India Office file reveal he proposed to Miss Parr and they were 'as much as engaged.' This appears to be the cause of his plan unravelling.

He came to the further attention of the India Office when Miss Parr called at Whitehall to say that Capt. F. J. Bibby had offered her an engagement as companion to a daughter of the Maharaja of Mysore; there is no detail on what made her visit Whitehall. Why call on her own; was she suspicious of this rather glib and confident Captain Bibby? The lady's brother-in-law called also, to say that Fred had told his sister the project had 'fallen through' and that he was no longer engaged to be married to his sister. This statement of Fred's and the visit of the brother-in-law appear in one of the police letters in the file. I assume that it was part of the police investigation and that he had been 'rumbled' by the brother before this visit by Miss Parr. This suggests that the brother went to the police, saying that Fred had described himself as a member of the Indian political Department and wasn't, which the brother now knew from his visit. It also suggests that Fred was then interviewed by the police and admitted he wasn't who he said he was; he was likely searched, the spurious business cards found, and he was arrested. Fred's statements to Miss Parr are not revealed in the documents, but they obviously aroused the suspicions of her family, so the brother-in-law had asked the India Office for verification of Fred's credentials, and then went to the police. So, although Fred could convince the Prime Minister of Mysore and came close to getting a British India Passport, he did not convince Miss Parr's family.

The Norwich police file did not survive, only their letters to the India Office, which don't mention how Miss Parr met Fred. Fred must have visited Norwich at some time while all this was all going on. Norwich would also be where Fred would flee to after he was rumbled and his world fell apart. From the evidence provided in this file, there is no doubt in my mind that Fred intended to marry Miss Parr and take her to India while still married to Grace. Did he woo her while still apparently residing in Lowestoft with Grace and her mother? How did he end up in Norwich when it appears to have started in a Russell Square Hotel? It's pretty clear from the file that he got the job in India, and very nearly, the girl.

Disappearing with a new persona was something I expect one could get away with then, as communication was not as swift as today. He could have just gone to India with this India Passport and his new wife. I am certain Grace did not know what he was about. What a rogue; but he would be a repeat offender.

I find it difficult to imagine what Grace and her mother thought he was doing in London while they languished in York House, I assume. Regardless of where they were, he must have told some story so as to absent himself to stay in the Imperial Hotel in Russell Square, and taken a large amount of money with him. Although the address on the letter requesting a commission in the Indian Army implies he resided in Lowestoft, his actual application for the commission said his permanent address was Forest Gate. So, in August 1920, Grace was living at York House and he at Forest Gate. Where did the money come from to fund what he was doing? He must have stayed in the Imperial Hotel for some time probably for at least a week or two during the Indian delegation visit, to maintain this deception. A local press report on his case states that he spent £1,200. That was a year's salary for some then. It also said that this money came from his mother, his mother-in-law, and his wife, so that must have been mentioned in court, as nothing is on the India File about it. Maybe he did visit Melbourne, like the returned prodigal, at some time between 1916 and 1920, to put the 'squeeze' on his mother for money. Was it ill-gotten gains from some other activity, or did he have a job after all?

Did Fred hope that the India Office would not connect this news of his engagement to this Miss Parr as a companion for his management position in Mysore with his application for an India Army commission as Captain Bibby DSC, and separate application for the British India passport? He was also masquerading as a Captain in the Australian Army to the Maharajah of Mysore's brother-in-law. So, all these activities were rattling around the India Office corridors. Strangely, due to bureaucracy perhaps, no one there had connected the dots together. But with the help of Miss Parr's brother, Inspector Nixon of the Norwich police soon put two and two together. And Fred found himself back in Lowestoft with Grace and an appointment at the Norwich Magistrate's Court of Petty Sessions in early November 1920.

9

REX Vs MR. F. J. BIBBY

The Norwich police told me that Fred's case file would have been destroyed. So exactly what happened on that day in court is unknown, as the solicitor's record is also lost to history. What remains is the record in a court register giving Fred's name, offence, date, and the fine. However, from the India Office file, I can reconstruct what happened in court and the outcome during those fateful closing days of Fred's grand deception. They had one of their officers of the Crown attend, as they had been asked by the police to witness the trial, and so had an observer at the event, and it was fortunate they did. Fred had been about to sail to India within the month when he was arrested and placed into custody. How close he got to his dream – he had got the job in Mysore and nearly sailed for India. He had a confirmed booking on a particular vessel on a specific date that same month. The all-important British India passport had been issued and was about to be delivered. The Maharajah's entourage had left some time ago, and were none the wiser. If he had not been arrested, he would have gone without Miss Parr, that was clear, and without Grace.

It was a close thing, from the India Office flurry of letters and memos that followed the trial. The response by the India Office seemed muted at first. Perhaps they felt that they had been duped by Fred, and were nervous about cooperating because of the poor reflection it might have cast on them. In the end, they had no choice, being asked to send a witness, but they reacted in an intriguing way. Their file paints somewhat of a different attitude towards Fred than the police took, and the press. What followed was a story of the execution of justice on one hand by the court system and a beguiling even-handedness on the part of some of the persons within the India Office – at very high levels, to boot. When I first read their correspondence, my intrigue began to build until I became bemused at the benign and open attitude expressed toward Fred and his deception, impersonating someone entirely different than what he was. I could only think that it was because the India Office evolved from the East India Company's civil service Indian connections. That company had long ceased to exist, but I suspected a cohort remained and acted almost as if they were a self-governed entity within the Foreign Office. Although the Company had disappeared, the people associated with it had come under the wing of the Foreign Office in Whitehall. These same people, perhaps with the same implanted independent attitudes and a more commercial nature than the ordinary civil servant, remained. Did that sense of 'British justice' so often mentioned by the downtrodden and disadvantaged in colonial parts of the empire during the Company's rule, still prevail in Fred's time? Nowhere in their letters is he called by any derogatory term. The wheels of justice were turning, but it wasn't Whitehall who was now deciding on Fred's future.

On November 8 1920, the Norwich Deputy Chief Constable, Richard Hodges, wrote to the India Office asking them to send a witness for the prosecution in the case against Fred. This was after a Detective Nixon from the Norwich Police, who ran the investigation into Fred's case, had visited earlier. Fred was now on remand, charged with contravening Defence of the Realm Regulation 45(g). This was no small misdemeanour. The charge was false representation by pretending to be a political officer in the Indian Civil Service. Under the section of the Act in question, he was liable to a maximum penalty of £100, or six months imprisonment with hard labour. I still wonder why the other impersonations represented by those bogus business cards were ignored. Perhaps the police went down the easiest path to ensure a successful prosecution.

Fred was looking at the likelihood of some serious time, unless he had £100, no small sum then. He had also been charged with attempted bigamy, but this was dropped by a prior agreement negotiated by his solicitor and the prosecution. The police request for a witness for the prosecution went up the line to Sir William Duke, the then Permanent Undersecretary for the State of the India Office. He was an ex-Governor of the State of Bengal who had become something of an icon in the India Service; words for posterity were recorded about him in the history of that office. So, Fred got the attention of not just a minor administrator. Clearly, some discussion between the India Office and the Chief Constable ensued, because the latter then sent another letter with an envelope found on Fred, addressed to a "Capt. Stephenson Bibby, York House, Victoria Road, Lowestoft." The use of another Christian name might suggest he had an alias, but that does not fit with his application; it remains unexplained. The Chief Constable's letter asked the India Office about how it came to be so addressed, and to Fred. Perhaps the India Office wanted some further evidence as to why they were being asked to be involved, and the Chief Constable provided it. It was lucky for them they got it, as if they hadn't, Fred likely would have got his desired India Passport!

The India Office sent a Mr. James A. Simpson to attend as a witness to report on Fred's planned new life in the Orient. Simpson's report on what happened in court appears as a hand-written 'minute' to the India Office file. He makes the point that he was attending the court under Sir Duke's 'instructions.' His report is detailed and very precise. Most of the other India Office correspondence is Dickensian in prose, in the vein of 'covering my backside' in some of the comments. Simpson didn't have to give evidence, as Fred had already pleaded guilty to the offence. He records that no attempt was made by Fred's solicitor to dispute any of the statements of fact made by the prosecution. In the course of the proceedings, various facts came to light which were not previously known to the India Office. They had not known that Fred was already married to Grace and therefore that he had come dangerously close to committing bigamy with Miss Parr. Also, the India Office had not known Fred had actually been appointed "Secretary and Manager of the Maharaja's Estates in Mysore" by the Maharaja's brother-in-law, one of the Maharajah's entourage of the Yuvaraja (son of the Maharaja) on that recent visit to London. Nor had they known that Fred had been busy for quite some time in London recruiting people for the Maharajah. They also had not known Fred had been authorised by the Maharajah's brother-in-law to advertise for positions like a governess and an assistant manager.

There must have been a dialogue between Fred and newspapers involving advertisements for these positions, and subsequent interviews, which opens up something of a Pandora's Box. Did he go to Norwich to interview Miss Parr, or she to London? Did he woo her and propose to her in Norwich? It says in the file they became engaged. The same applies to the assistant manager position. So, Fred had the authority to do all these things, but he just wasn't who he said he was. Fred had been given a wide scope to act on the Maharajah's behalf through this brother-in-law, which I found extraordinary. Fred had gone a long way to convincing a number of people that he was capable and his deception was well on the way to being successful. And he apparently had money left over to pay for a solicitor. He appears to have been well briefed to take a remorseful stand. His solicitor confined himself to a sob story about him and appealed to the magistrates that it was indeed a case of 'ad misericordiam' – a legal Latin term for a plea for pity under special circumstances. Fred must have known the game was up when he found a policeman on his doorstep at York House, and perhaps contrived to appear as the misguided young man with a war injury. I doubt he was sincere about that; as will be shown he had plans to flee and probably was looking for a fine and doing a runner. The solicitor emphasised Fred's youth, which was given as twenty-two, which was correct. How that was established, though, without a certificate and with an army form saying he was older puzzled me.

The solicitor also mentioned Fred's service in the war as a private with the Australian forces in Gallipoli and the fact that he was suffering from shellshock. He says he could not prove Fred's statement that he suffered from shellshock, and that he had only the defendant's word for it, but stated "there could be little doubt of the truth of the fact." This means Fred did not reveal to anybody his discharge certificate as it clearly says that was his condition on discharge. Nor his medical record, nor that prestigious 'Kings Certificate,' which was a surprise, as there is a clear record he got it. So he kept his reason for discharge to himself, it seems. I can only guess he did not reveal it because he was still ashamed of it. Or because the certificate stated he was older than he truly was, and if the court believed that, they might not have been so lenient. So, he told his own sob story to the solicitor, who believed him. Simpson's 'minute' to his superiors, reporting from the trial, described Fred in the dock as "one quivering, trembling mass of nerves." He wrote that he believed that it was shellshock he was still suffering from. So here was support from an unexpected quarter. The solicitor stressed that Fred was sailing on the 19 November to take up his appointment in Mysore. This is despite the fact that he had been shown to be a bogus Captain Bibby, which didn't seem to matter to his solicitor, or anybody else, which I thought odd. Simpson also stated it was clear Fred's solicitor set great store by Fred's impending departure for India to take up his position, with the "greatest stress of all" which was the flag from Simpson to his superiors that the India Office needed to act further.

Fred's recruited Mysore Estate Assistant Manager was in court as a witness and is also mentioned in Simpson's 'minute' to Sir Duke. He describes him as "even less than Bibby himself, as an individual competent to hold a position in a Native State which would appear to be one of considerable importance." Was he an accomplice to Fred's deception? Perhaps he was an ex-private soldier mate, recently discharged like him. Or someone he teamed up with in his round of hospitalisation. Who was this Assistant Manager, and did he also have the required passport? I could not find out who he was. His name would have been in that destroyed police case file that is now lost to history. Providing he didn't get a custodial sentence, Fred, with the support of his solicitor, was still expecting to get his Indian passport and go to India. It seems hard to believe as he clearly had failed to qualify in all respects, as well as nearly becoming a bigamist. His solicitor implored the magistrates not to blight his future career by a sentence of imprisonment, but to impose a fine which would be paid and would allow the defendant to sail as arranged for India, where he had every prospect of leading "a happy and honoured life." His solicitor must have been damned good and it is regrettable the trial record is lost. Anyway, the magistrate agreed and imposed a fine of £10 and £10.5.6 costs.

Fred clearly paid his fine, breathed a sigh of relief, and may have scarpered home to York Terrace to face Grace and his mother-in-law. Or did he? Well, he still thought he had a job and a ship to catch and was getting a British India passport! He would have to act fast. The word was getting around and not only in the India Office in Whitehall, with Simpson's warning about Fred's 'impending departure' for India. And there was that British India passport already on its way to him. The local press were present at the trial; two articles appeared in the *London Observer* and *Daily Chronicle,* both London dailies of the time, on the day following the trial. The story would be passed on to their syndicated press in Australia. So, it was public knowledge in England immediately after the trial, and very soon would be in Australia. At the same time, the people in Whitehall went into a sort of 'panic mode.'

10

THE INDIA OFFICE Vs FRED

The local press articles were followed closely by a frenzy of activity in the India Office. Hand-written memos and draft letters flew sideways between desk officers and up and down between them and lords of the realm, all trying to decide how to deal with a chastised, but not chastened, free agent Fred, with 'I am still going to India" on his mind. The information that he still intended to sail for Mysore and take up the position as Estate Manager really put the 'cat amongst the pigeons' at Whitehall. It is only the India Office that still believed he had this intent though, as the police saw it as a closed case. Throughout, it appears that the Mysore delegation were completely unaware of what had transpired in the Norwich court. The times, with their less efficient communications than we see today, were working in Fred's favour.

It started with a letter from the Departmental Secretary, Mr. J. Shuckburgh, a career India Office man who would end up much later with a knighthood for his services to the Crown. After the court proceedings, advised of the conclusion of the case by the Chief Constable, he wrote to Sir Charles Bayley of the Foreign Office and recently returned ex-Governor of Bombay. It appeared that responsibilities between these departments overlapped, but they were all no doubt from the same India service cohort. On 11 November, Shuckburgh wrote seeking Sir Bayley's advice on a "rather unusual case" as he called it. They were now aware from the court case report by their Simpson that he still had plans to sail there before the end of November. The immediate point for consideration, he wrote, was whether the India Office ought not to intervene, or prevent "Capt. Bibby from sailing for India on the 19th."

Did it not matter that he was acting still as a bogus military officer? This was a surprise to read, but also to find that they still referred to him as Captain Bibby, after what had been revealed in the Norwich court. What is even more surprising is that they were inclined not to prevent him going. Perhaps the reasoning was that he had been punished for the impersonation as a political officer, but he still had the position as a manager. In what followed, he stated that he thought there was no case to punish him further and that they, the India Office took the view that there was no question of any obligation to further protect Fred's prospective employer, the Maharaja, as Fred's case has been before the Courts, and was consequently in the public domain. In other words, the Maharaja's brother-in-law or any other related Indian interest could read about it in the press anyway.

He goes on to state they are not bound to call the employer's attention to the matter when there is nothing to prevent the Maharaja from finding out for himself. He wrote that "it is not as if Bibby were entering the service of the Mysore

State." His argument is that Fred's employer is a private individual who is presumably entitled, if he chooses to do so, to employ an agent of doubtful "antecedents." He covers himself by stating there is the obvious political objection to letting "dubious Europeans get a footing in Native States." But, he says, considering everything, he was inclined to "give Bibby his chance." He suggests taking no further action beyond forwarding the papers "demi-officially," whatever that means – probably like passing an unmarked brown envelope between departments. I took that to mean telling the Secretary of State for India in the Foreign Office unofficially. So, this seemed to me a case of not wanting the India Office to be further involved, or its name dragged down with Fred, more likely.

Sir Bayley came back with the advice that if the Maharaja, through his brother-in-law, knew as much about Fred as the India Office, he knew it would be unlikely he would employ him. He agreed that it was likely he, the Maharaja would find out anyway through the publicity. He says they should send the 'papers' to the Maharaja in Mysore. He also says they should write to Fred and tell him they have done so and that he travels to India at his own risk. This seems to be all classic 'cover your backside stuff' to me. But it didn't end there for the India Office, as they received a letter a couple of days later from the Chief Constable's office. This letter contained some pretty damning information about Fred, including details of his past history and career. It highlights the many false statements in his application for a commission. Importantly, it gave the name of the shipping line he was planning to travel to India with on November 19, a Clan Line Steamer. Further correspondence between the India Office and the shipping line revealed the vessel was the *S.S. Clan Mc Taggart*, leaving from Liverpool on November 20, and Fred is listed as a passenger. So, the India Office had to act, as the clock was ticking on the India passport issue. As well as letters to and from the shipping Company, there follows a flurry of memos, with words like "time is short," a draft letter to Fred advising of the consequences if he leaves for India, and an annotation "issue at once." But then it was not sent.

Whilst all this was going on, Fred got his passport for India, which was issued on 15 November from the Chief Passport Officer (CPO), St James Park SW1. So, there was a bureaucratic disconnection somewhere that allowed this to happen. Fred was very nearly on his way. The India Office found out – how is not clear – and a very cryptic memo stamped 'Immediate' was sent to the CPO telling him to withdraw the passport immediately. In the sideline note on file there is a detailed description by a Mr. Wakely from the India Office, who must have gone to the passport office to find out how it happened. This part of the saga ends with a letter from the shipping company, Cayzer, Irvine & Co Ltd (Clan Line Steamers) acknowledging the fact that Fred's passport had been withdrawn by their advice and that they had advised him he was unable to sail from Liverpool on the *Clan Mc Taggart* on 20 November. It was a close thing and Fred very nearly got away with it.

Did the India Office send the papers on to the Maharaja anyway, and thus ensure the door was finally closed on Fred's India adventure? The final correspondence involved a Sir John Ward, Political Secretary of the Foreign & Political Department, who sent a telegram to the Viceroy in Retamilla India advising about Fred and his "highly unsatisfactory record." He added that the papers on him were in the mail and he may take what action he sees necessary, or do nothing at all, as he hints at the end. Was that an attempt to bury any embarrassment for issuing Fred his India Passport? And what about that passport, did he still have it, but could not use it, for India anyway? Apparently not, but it would transpire that he still had a regular one.

The India Office file ends with a draft letter to Fred, to his York House address, drawing his attention to the court proceedings, his intent to go to India, that his prospective employer had been advised, and that if he proceeded to India he did so at his own risk. It asked that he acknowledge the letter. It is a handwritten draft and there is no typed copy, so I cannot know if it was finally sent or if he replied. I wondered if he ever got that letter. I would say Fred would have been keeping a very low profile in the Norwich area by this time rather than go back to Grace. Grace surely would be there and know it all by this time. Somewhere during this particular phase, maybe he did communicate, as there is a note that he told the India Office he was now going to Singapore to see his family. He could travel, as he still had his regular passport, but it was now marked 'not valid for India.'

He did have family in Singapore – three family graves he could visit. And an Uncle Arthur, his deceased father's younger brother, living the life of a plantation owner, still mining in Pahang near Raub, where his father's grave lay. At the Bukit Timah cemetery in the Anglican section, his paternal great-grandfather and great-grandmother, William and Amelia, and his uncle, his father's oldest brother, William Charles, were buried. Saying he was going to Singapore suggests to me that he did meet up with Nellie and her family. If his mother didn't tell him that family story, Nellie would have. But then again, maybe saying he was returning to Singapore to see his family was just part of the tapestry of his new persona as the merchant with the mythical fourteen years growing up in the East. His uncle Arthur in Singapore, miner, planter, and merchant, could have probably given him some sound advice on that score.

He had a large family looking in on his misadventures. The London newspapers were obviously syndicated with some press in Australia, as Fred's folly was well reported at home. Reports appeared in January through February 1921 in *The Register* and *The Journal* in Adelaide, The *Daily Standard* in Brisbane, and in the Sydney regional papers, the *Maitland Daily Mercury* and the *Richmond River Herald*. But it did not appear in Melbourne. So his own close and large family in that city may not have known what happened to him, at the time anyway. The headings ranged from BLOWN UP AT GALLIPOLI, SWELLED HEAD, LOVER WHO POSED AS A CAPTAIN, to AUSTRALIAN'S YARNS TO A NORWICH GIRL.

I feel certain that his uncle Phillip in Adelaide would have seen at least one of them. Phillip Edward was his father's youngest brother who had settled in Adelaide after coming back from Malaya. Phillip also served in WWI in France and returned unscathed. He might have given a wry grin when he saw it and even kept quiet about it for his own reasons. Phillip was born in 1886so he was in his thirties when he went to war. Before the war, from all accounts, he struggled to find his niche in life and got involved in Labor politics and what looked like branch stacking, and found himself in court like Fred. It got him mentioned in Parliament so he had his moment in the limelight too. So, he might have seen Fred as a kindred spirit, in a way.

Was Fred waiting in Liverpool to catch his ship soon after the trial? And where was Grace during all of this? Grace was present at York house during the trial, so she now knew he was planning to go to India without her. It must have been hard for her to bear, let alone it being now public news. It is hard to believe the marriage surviving after what transpired, age difference aside. The mother-in-law's presence throughout the marriage, as mentioned in the press, was not unusual. Maybe Mrs Lambert senior still saw Fred as the bread winner, saving her eldest daughter from becoming a spinster, and held it together. But the role of Miss Parr in it all suggests that Fred was unfaithful in intent and forethought, regardless of how far that potential match progressed before it all got to court. He will return to Grace, but the marriage will not last, and not just because of what happened in Norwich in November 1920. Norwich, not a great distance away from there, some twenty miles north, would be where he would gravitate next, surprisingly, considering what transpired there.

11

BETWEEN THE WARS

Here he was at the end of 1920, revealed as a fake with the public disgrace of the trial and press reports locally and at home. At least he did not end up in jail. So where did he go now? Could he still stay with Grace and her mother-in-law after what he had done became public in the London popular dailies of the time? I wondered if Nellie and her husband had seen the newspaper reports, although *The Times* was more likely their type of newspaper. His career had soared into the limelight and burned just as quickly. But I have to remind myself he didn't break-in or steal anything, no one really got hurt, and I will assume even Miss Parr survived her encounter with him. Private F.J. Bibby had convinced some important dignitaries, the Prime Minister of Mysore and his entourage, that he was somebody entirely different than he really was. No doubt now he had acquired a taste for the high life and hobnobbing in a social class that a boy from St Arnaud might not have expected. He might have taken strength from that achievement and thought optimistically, well next time!

Reflecting on Fred's life so far: was he just a rogue, or a misguided young man lacking a father or mother's advice? Putting aside the outcome and obvious fraudulent behaviour, it was quite an achievement for a country lad with no more than a high school education. He very nearly became a Maharajah's right-hand man. Think of what he had to do to fool so many people! He must have displayed some presence and conviction that he was what he said he was. I had only just left the army apprentices' school at his age and could not imagine doing the same, by any stretch of my imagination. Did his war experience, brief as it was, make him older than his years? And coincidence arrives again. When I was in England for training in 1969 and his Aunt Nellie was still alive, an authentic Captain Bibby with the Queens Commission stayed in Russell Square at a more modern hotel Imperial, the embassy choice for Officers passing through London then. And, like Fred, I married an English girl, but a younger one than Grace. We returned together to Australia when my duty was done, unlike Fred. I wonder now about how our separate paths crossed so many years ago in another generation, but for decidedly different reasons and on different missions, of course. I doubt I would have been able to display such self-belief, even then. Like him, I grew up without a father, albeit still living, but an absent one. But you could say I had been walking in his footsteps again.

I do not know if Fred returned to Grace at this time, although she must have known he had been in London, but not what he was up to. The Forest Gate house may have still been owned by her mother, as it is quoted as one of Fred's addresses during the trial. I am guessing that was most likely true, and probably much of his lifestyle up till now might have been partly funded by Grace's family. Women of that period in such a position had few rights compared to today; she was still married to him. And of those few rights, none allowed that she could refuse to have her legal husband back, and she might have accepted it as her plight – if, indeed, he ever lived in York House before or while his deception was going on. Before his deception was discovered, when Grace and her mother had moved there from Forest Gate, he was probably mostly in London or Norwich. I suspect he may have just used the address at York House like a mail drop to pick up his mail from the India Office, as he had given that address for that India passport.

For all that, after the trial, I believe he left Grace and went to ground in London or thereabouts, as he had more plans. Fred did leave England, as the India Office said, but it wasn't to go to Singapore, and not immediately. If he had stayed in Lowestoft with Grace before he left for Australia it was only for a short while, and he spent most his time in London. He was very familiar with that place by now and knew where he could find a bolt hole. What he did in England in those two years after his conviction seems to have disappeared from the public records. He had definite travel plans though, and a reason to visit Australia. He had another reason to return apart from seeing his family; he went looking for something the army owed him, his gratuity.

Fred left the Port of London on April 22 1922 on the S.S. *Moreton Bay*. She was a brand new P&O ship which later would be sold to the Australian Commonwealth Line and carried a mix of passengers and freight, and later, paying migrants to Australia. Perhaps just by chance, this ship will loom large in his life much later. The ship's passenger log shows his full name and an indecipherable London address in WC2. He describes himself as a 'farm worker'; his Grandfather James Brain might have smiled at that. It's an odd combination of address and occupation. So, he did finally leave Grace in Lowestoft after the trial and ended up in London and in the West End, which he had frequented before, a considerable step up from Forest Gate in the Romford Road area. He could have gone to visit his Aunt Nellie, assuming he had established that connection. But if Nellie was linked to Fred in any way, he would not want to be seeing her at this time. He was alone on this voyage, so there was not another Miss Parr involved. In third class, so no reason to pretend to be someone other than he really was.

The ship was bound for Brisbane, but he ended up in Melbourne. His mother was living at Alma Road, Caulfield, Melbourne at this stage. William Raub had returned from the war unscathed and was still at the same bank in Melbourne, and twin brother Arthur still doing his Pharmacy studies. Annie would die two years later in Caulfield of breast cancer after three years' illness. So, she must have been ill while he visited; was this the main reason for this visit? If so, were there letters or a telegram, perhaps, that called him back? It looks like he may have had another reason to return. Annie was now fifty-nine and still lamenting her loss of Fred's father, Frederick Alfred. She would place yearly tributes to him in the obituary column of *The Argus* on the anniversary of his death until she died. She clearly had loved Fred's father dearly and mourned that they had so little time together, some eight years only. She became very close to her late husband's older brother, Harry, who also lived in Melbourne. They are buried alongside each other in Brighton Cemetery. She loved her children just as much, I expect, and maybe forgave Fred for his prodigal ways; she would leave him £500 in her will, not an insignificant sum then.

Annie bequeathed the elder son the house in Caulfield that she had named Raub, after the town in Malaya that figured so much in Fred's family history. That nameplate, still in the family, can be found in a Gippsland town, another signpost to Fred's life, like those honour rolls in St Arnaud and that memorial at Beazeleys Bridge. Fred's twin would get the funds to finish his pharmacy studies. Both these sons remained in Melbourne until their deaths, living ordinary lives, without the wanderlust of Fred. His older brother William and his wife Eileen would have no offspring, and on Fred's behest, as part of some plan he was hatching concerning us that never bore fruit, would visit us at Swan in the early 1950s. I only know this visit happened from a faded photograph, but have no memory of it. William died in Caulfield in 1978 aged eighty-five, and Arthur, the other brother, in 1994 at ninety-six, both of natural causes. Although I would stay with Arthur during my years in the army in Melbourne, soon after leaving Swan, both their deaths passed by unknown to me at the time, showing the effect of my upbringing. Extended family and what it meant came much later in my life, and not until I had children of my own. Much like Fred, as it happened.

Fred was home for a number of months. His return voyage does not show in any record I could find, but something else tells me where he was and how long he stayed. Whilst in Melbourne, he visited the Army Headquarters, as he was seeking his war bond from the War Gratuity Department in Melbourne. His visit appears on a notation about him on a file that had been raised relating to an enquiry to the Repatriation Department by Grace. Grace had written to the army in Melbourne on the advice of Australia House, asking about him. Her enquiry occurred not long after he had left for Australia and it suggests that Fred did finally leave Grace after the trial for a period, and even when he got back, he may not have returned to her. He wasn't at York House late in 1922. She had written that letter to Australia on 11 October that year. This letter suggests that Fred was not living with her at the time, and from her words, she knew he had gone home. The letter did not ask where he was, only if he had taken up any land under the Soldier Settlement Scheme. It shows she still considered herself his legal wife and was due any entitlements, and it was a means of tracking his whereabouts, of course. So, Grace knew a thing or two about Australia and how it treated its soldiers after the war. Did Fred spin a yarn to her about what the future could mean for them, a life on the land maybe, in St Arnaud, under the soldier settlement scheme?

The chances of Fred ending up back on the farm, though, were next to nothing by now, I would think.

A copy of Grace's October 1922 letter went the rounds of all the states, asking if Fred had applied for a land grant. That notation about a visit by Fred appeared on the Melbourne file copy of a Queensland Department of Repatriation memorandum reply to the Melbourne headquarters, saying he hadn't taken up land in Queensland. The hand-written notation gives an address in St Kilda Melbourne; it is initialled and dated December 12 1922, and says he had dropped in a couple of days ago. So, that pretty well establishes he was still in Melbourne in December 1922. It also says he applied for his bond; a sum of six pounds fifteen shillings, which Treasury had paid to him on August 2 1922. Somewhat at odds to his signing everything away in London, I thought, but he was entitled to it, after all. The army didn't pass the information about Fred's visit on to Grace, even though it occurred well before her inquiry, when they wrote directly to her on January 25 1923 telling her he had not applied for any land grant. So she may not have known about his bond payment, such as it was, but it's clear she did know he had gone to Australia.

I venture Fred didn't realise that, due to observant clerks and a bureaucratic penchant for keeping records, he would leave a trace of his past for all to see later. I puzzled over the St Kilda address. His mother's house was substantial; why not that address? It seems he was welcome, judging by his inheritance when she died. In that image of the brothers, he appears the right age for it to have been taken around this time; if so, they were together as a family. Perhaps he was just making sure his visit to the army was for him only to know and not his family. But what do we really know about Fred and this part of his life anyway? A marriage he hid from all his family then, and later, from his children. He now had a criminal record. Might he want to conceal that?

I found no evidence that Fred returned to Grace in Lowestoft on his arrival back in England from Australia by the end of 1922. I found no shipping record, but he did return of course. It seems to me now that he considered England home. Long-suffering Grace, still in Lowestoft, by the timing of her October letter to Australia, was unlikely to be the first on his visit list by this time, given the disgraceful way he had treated her so far. But she was still his wife and he had obligations, despite the marital rules at that time weighing heavily in the husband's favour. Before the India Office trial, Grace was likely oblivious to the fact that Fred was using his charms elsewhere on Miss Parr, and was completely unaware of his actual activities in London. There may have been some contact after the trial, as she knew he had gone to Australia. On his disappearance again and to Australia, she may have suspected he was up to no good again.

There was no farm waiting for Grace in Australia, or a future for her there. If Fred had turned up at any time after his return from Australia she would probably have taken him back, considering the times. But the marriage was doomed to fail, as Fred would be using his charms elsewhere again very soon. From the act of writing to the authorities, Grace clearly showed an interest in him still, but it may have been in desperation. His London address before sailing to Australia shows that there was probably some long period of separation at this time. His failure to remain by her side permanently now must have been as big a shock as the India Office affair. By this time, Fred had found his niche as a travelling salesman, as we will see. Clearly he had a way about him and could sell himself. It is obvious that Fred was more than aware of this appeal and utilised it when it came to wooing that Miss Parr. By now Fred still had the idea that he was meant for greater things than remaining wed to a much older Grace, and living at York house with perhaps a mother-in-law in tow. His operating area was mostly in Suffolk, judging by what happened next. I was unable to find any record of where Fred was until later when he ended up in Ipswich. There is no record of him travelling overseas again but that doesn't mean he didn't. Did he do a spell on the *Moreton Bay* as crew, as he would later?

It appears from what happens next he had moved to Ipswich and later, according to Grace, was living with her. He definitely seems to have remained in communication with her or visited or even stayed with her during his travels in his new role as a salesman, or for whatever other reason, maybe even to give her money, as she seemed to know what he was up to. If that were true, he had some sense of duty of care, regardless of what he really felt. They had remained married and during those times of course, Fred could make demands Grace couldn't refuse. I find it difficult to imagine a young, dashing Fred, the salesman, still in his mid-twenties, and an aging Grace. This period was a long one, until things between them came to a sudden end. During the twenty or so between-war years, I cannot account for what Fred actually continued to do in his work and personal life; but what documents there are suggest he was with Grace, a salesman and based in Ipswich.

It was near the end of this time he met Daphne Ada, only child of Leonard and Elizabeth Bellamy of Romford. I do not know exactly how or when Fred met Daphne; he never told me, and I never asked him. I did ask her once about Fred when I was a young man, but the memories for her were too bitter for her to respond in any meaningful way, and I learned nothing. When Fred met her, she must have been at most twenty-one. He was forty or forty-one and had spent the interwar years it seems, as a travelling salesman in Suffolk. The age situation was reversed this time; Daphne was a very attractive, dark-haired beauty and just as tall as Fred, from memory. Maybe it was his well-polished and self-confident ways, and he came across as a man of the world. By the late 30s, they were clearly together, living as man and wife.

Daphne did not come from a well-to-do family; her father was a clerk in Inland Revenue and later, had something to do with the music business; Daphne was musical, from what she left behind when she died. Perhaps Fred might have sold them something, perhaps furniture for their new house in

Carter Drive Romford, where Daphne was born; they lived here after moving from Surrey. Perhaps they met in Ipswich, where Daphne seemed to gravitate later. Fred was definitely a furniture salesman by this time. I am certain he had a decent wage, a better one than some of the working middle class. Between the wars was a time when mass production of household goods gave a sense of respectability to a middle class much in need of it. So, he was in the right profession for those times. However, it was not long before Grace found out about Daphne.

What happened next suggests that Daphne had taken up a lot of Fred's time and Grace had had enough. Grace's divorce proceedings confirm Daphne was twenty-one at the time she met Fred. Daphne was obviously in Ipswich, as that is where they met a number of times, according to the record. Fred was still selling furniture and I can only suppose still acting the husband to Grace. He probably met Daphne socially; Ipswich is the only place I recall my mother talking about. Later records show her living and working there, so maybe it was 'her town' to go to for fun. Maybe Fred's sophistication and promises and grand plans, which she would refer to later, led her to believe he would provide the 'good life.'

My memories of when I was a child with my mother are of a softly spoken woman with a neutral 'English accent,' certainly not the one from the Essex I know from having worked for some time at Stanstead Airport after leaving the army. Strangely, I was also in a selling role, but aircraft maintenance, not furniture like Fred. I can add little else as to how they got together and about their later relationship before it all came crashing down again for Fred, when a disillusioned Daphne left him after a short time, with four children in tow, two out of wedlock. Daphne's words to me much later are telling, though. She visited me when I was living with my growing family in New Guinea after I had left the army. I had not seen her since I had left Swan some forty years earlier. Even then, she had not mellowed and did not want to talk about her life with Fred. To her, as I recall from any attempt at conversation on the subject, he was a 'liar and a fraud' and generally a 'bad man.' So I would say he spun her stories about himself and what he had planned similar to those he told Grace away back in the beginning.

In my memory of Fred, he had a morbid fear of being called working class. I can hear him now in his polished accent saying that well worn phrase; 'it's not what you know but who you know.' I don't recall he ever spoke 'strine' or with any hint of an Australian accent. And I daresay he never went further north than Ipswich or west of Cambridge, let alone Mesopotamia or India. Nor did he have, I think, any opinion, or even idea, of what life was like in the industrial north of England. He wasn't a merchant from the east, but he was a furniture salesman. He was listed as such in the divorce papers that came from Grace. Daphne was listed as the co-respondent.

12

A DIVORCE

Grace's application for a divorce for Fred's alleged adultery with Daphne was lodged at Norwich High Court of Justice on December 9 1936. So, Fred could be headed for that Norwich court again. The 'show cause' date was set down for February 11 1937. This shows she meant business and had had enough of his unreliability and infidelity. It was a time when mutual agreement for divorce was not acceptable. It was here that I would begin to really feel for Grace, as she seemed to disappear into obscurity. She had succoured him in his time of 'illness,' despite what one might think of her prospects then of life as a spinster. She must have had sincere feelings then, even if they were not returned on Fred's side. She seems to have stood by him through the ignominy of his trial and then his scarpering off to Australia while she led a prosaic life with her mother in Lowestoft. How ironic though for Fred, that he was being told to return to the town of his earlier shame for the divorce hearing. It was over seventeen years since those events. But I would think he had a pretty thick skin by this time.

The petition states that Grace and Fred were living at 12 Bucklesham Road, Ipswich and had lived there until the time of the divorce case. This was some evidence to me that she may have taken him back after his escapade to

Australia in 1922. Well, likely she had no choice, unless she had independent means, which seems unlikely, particularly as Fred, according to the press, spent a large sum of her funds. It suggests they may have lived together all that time after he came back until Daphne came along. He was the breadwinner, as was mostly normal in those days, and Grace, I assume, would not have worked, and wanted nothing other than a faithful husband to provide for her. Of course, there was the Great Depression during that time and it would have been hard times selling furniture, perhaps. They had also gone through the roaring twenties with its particular new type of social behaviour; no doubt Fred cut a dashing figure despite his smallish stature and was always smartly dressed. He had a wardrobe to impress. from his earlier escapades. He was in his mid-twenties with his life in England back on track, cash from his mother's will, and surely with lingering grand dreams. He still had a head of hair, like me when I was in my early thirties, but the thinning signs were appearing. I would have his genes in that regard.

Daphne, the very much younger woman, was the final straw for Grace. In the divorce petition record, Grace had employed help to make her case, and a Westminster Lawyers agent no less to deliver the petitions. This didn't look like a divorce due to adultery by mutual consent, as was sometimes the case. It became obvious that Fred had left Grace to be with Daphne some months before all this happened. The divorce papers suggest that he was caught 'in flagrante delicto'; the detail is very precise. The petition states that the 'Respondent habitually committed adultery with Daphne Bellamy' between March and August. After that he had left Grace and until October 1936 he was living with Daphne at 39 St Helen's Street in Ipswich. Grace had someone employed to make a solid case, from the amount of detail she gathered, and Fred didn't stand a chance of denying anything. By the time the papers were served, Fred was living at the Grosvenor Hotel, Berners Street Ipswich. I was stunned to find the same building and with the same name and in use in Ipswich today. In 2020, it looks freshly painted and still bears its name and is a hotel. But, even in its day, it was a far cry as an establishment and location from its West End namesake. It looks to me like a typical commercial hotel of the period that travelling salesmen would inhabit while on the road.

By this time, Fred was not living with Grace or with Daphne, which says a lot about his intentions of marriage after Grace. Grace had even obtained Daphne's residential address, 45 Bixley Road Ipswich, also extant. A notice was served there and demanded she appear in court. Daphne was renting this house and so likely working in Ipswich. The record also states that Fred was a 'travelling salesman' and that he committed adultery 'numerous times' and during weekends in March through August 1936 at two different places. The addresses given in the divorce papers are 60 and 64 Fitzroy Street Cambridge, hotels or lodging places, perhaps. So obviously Daphne was travelling with

Fred at times on his sales trips! One can still find the addresses. The buildings are replaced and in the centre of the city. Only Daphne is cited in the application, which suggests Fred was loyal to her, at least. Without a doubt, Grace had employed a private investigator to obtain such precise information, and her case was watertight.

I had difficulty putting Daphne into any sort of social set in these between-war years. She appeared to have no qualifications. Later, she will be described officially as a domestic. Did Fred tell her he was from Australia and about his Gallipoli experience? Did he have plans to take her home to Australia, or did he even tell her about his big family there? Later correspondence from another world and time shows that she knew nothing about his Australian family. Perhaps she was a means to an end for him, to get out of a failed marriage. That marriage was dissolved and Grace's decree nisi was granted on June 8 1937.

I can write little more about Grace; she seemed to be a patient and long-suffering soul. If that sounds condescending, it is not meant so. Grace was a kind of crutch for Fred during his darkest days after the first war and for that and her patience with him, she must be blessed. Her mother too, for writing that letter to her friend in Melbourne, for how else would I know so much? Grace lived until aged 86 and I fear might have died alone without a family like Fred had when he died. She died in Colchester in 1968, the year before I arrived as that authentic Captain Bibby, about fifty miles south from where Nellie, Fred's aunt, was living at the time, in Bungay in Suffolk, just after her husband had died. Like some web of fate only fifteen miles west of Lowestoft. Nellie, with her extended family, did not die alone, not much later in 1972.

This part is only a reflection on Fred's life. Much that I discovered about him made him hard to like. The divorce's revelations made me think Fred was, in the parlance of the time, just an old-fashioned cad during this period of his life. He didn't seem to care about the people he hurt. Why did he marry Grace in the first place, to make a family, or he was just in love, aged eighteen? If he knew how old she was, was he too young to understand what that meant in regard to children? He would have them later with Daphne without restraint, wed or not. And what about Daphne, was she that naïve? To like him, though, was essential for me, but waiting for the sweet stuff would be a long wait. A photograph found among his possessions after his death is at a Bromley church. It dates from the mid-1940s, and shows a dapper Fred on the right of a youngish couple. He's wearing a very fashionable suit for that time. Was the gentleman getting married his cohort in the Mysore affair, or just a business colleague from his 'merchant' activities during the second war, soon to come? I had thought it might have lead to a Nellie connection, but it didn't, and who the couple were remains a mystery. As the photo came from his last possessions, they likely were important people in his life. The image is always how I will remember him. The church is named St Marys, common enough in the Anglican Church, like the one of the same name in my story to follow.

13

CHILDREN, MARRIAGE AND SEPARATION

Children, marriage and separation, in that order, because that is how it happened. At this time in Fred's life, another world war was not far away, but there was optimism in the air and he was probably doing alright for himself selling furniture. He had no concerns about being involved in any further conflict. He was many miles away from those who knew of him and his past. Maybe he felt his encounter with war, brief as it was, was quite enough, and he likely focussed more on his personal situation and of course, the current relationship with Daphne, someone nearly half his age. The public mood in Britain then about what was happening in Germany was that it wouldn't affect them at home, and the political mood was that it would be 'peace in our time.' But not domestically for Fred, it would transpire! In February 1937 Fred had submitted willingly to his divorce from Grace; she had not yet received her decree absolute, so he wasn't quite a free agent in terms of re-marriage. But that did not stop him from starting a new family. He had now moved in with Daphne at 39 St Helena St. Ipswich, one of those addresses given in the divorce petition. They must have given the impression they were now man and wife, as demanded by the strong social mores at the time. As a travelling salesman, his patch seemed to stretch from

Cambridge in the west to all of Norfolk and probably all of Essex. Apart from the court costs, there was no settlement, so he had no financial burden other than taking care of himself – he was well practised in that – and taking care of Daphne, of course.

Daphne was, at the very least, six months pregnant when she moved in with him. He was thirty-nine and she was twenty-one. However, they were now giving the appearance to landlord and all that they were married. Donald James was born on March 24 1937 at Helena Street. Fred's occupation had not changed; he was still a furniture salesman and Daphne is listed as a domestic. The name Donald must have come from Daphne, as all our names would, as none appear in Fred's family ancestry. At some time after Donald's birth, they moved to another address a long way from Ipswich – to south-east London; it was called 'The View,' Kinsale Road, Camberwell. This is south of the river and not that far from Bromley and St Marys church. Most of the street from that period is extant and includes their house. It shows that in their time, it was a fashionable, middle-class area. Fred was a successful furniture salesman, judging by that address. Grace's decree absolute was issued in February 1938 and my sister born on 28 June that year. That year passed and into 1939 and they remained unwed and had had another child. They were still living at Kinsale Road at the time.

What was Fred thinking about this growing family he was responsible for? His actions to date were quite reprehensible, as perhaps to some extent were Daphne's.

Although was she was probably misled by Fred's promises? Why did the philanderer and his co-respondent not marry, now the coast was clear to do so? Brutal words I know, but as this was revealed to me (I had never known it before) I became angry at Fred, as I dug deeper trying to find reasons for his behaviour. Was it him or her that did not wish to yet marry? But why go on having children; was Daphne naïve or perhaps ignorant of her choices in the matter? Was it Daphne who, despite having children, did not wish to marry this older man? Did she really love him? Impossible questions to answer now. I wonder now if Daphne knew who Fred really was, other than this older, debonair and worldly Englishman who claimed to speak Eastern languages and maybe talked of past business interests in the same way as before, just a story he made up. Did he tell her only the good bits of that experience? I suspect he might have.

What about Daphne's parents? Was there any pressure from them, or did they see her as a fallen woman now who had run off with a man nearly twice her age? It was the brink of war again, with all its uncertainty and that might have contributed to the situation. But Fred's presence wasn't uncertain, so it was unlikely to have been because of the war. They did finally marry while still living at Kinsale Road; it was at the Camberwell Registry Office on Aug 31 1940 with another world war already underway, and another child. I cannot know what made Fred and Daphne finally legitimise their relationship in a marriage, or what forced his hand. Daphne was some few months pregnant with the third child when they married. On the marriage certificate, Fred called himself a shift leader in the Ambulance Service, and working as an ARP (Air Raid Warden). With all the other previous untruths about him on certificates, I hoped that was true when I read it. Whether it was his real occupation is moot, when the third child followed he called himself a 'Manufacturer's Agent' in the record.

My older brother was born some four months after the marriage, on 21 December 1940. His second name came from Daphne's father, so was there a family reconciliation of sorts with her mother and father, since they had at last tied the knot? Fred and Daphne had now moved to Romford in north east London and are shown living at 26 Carter Drive on that birth certificate. Just down the road from our grandparents, Leonard and Elizabeth. So, it seemed Fred had settled down to domesticity and all he had to do was to survive the bombing, continue making a living, and bring up his family. Presumably now in England, as Australia didn't seem to be on the horizon. Fred was incorrigible, it seems to me now; he had another occupation, a manufacturer's agent as well as selling furniture, apart from his claimed war duties as an ARP. As far as an agent goes, I can imagine all sorts of things being manufactured and opportunities for Fred with his quick mind and gregarious nature as the war ramped up, but I can only guess at what Fred could have been selling with his background. During the period between wars, despite the Great Depression, Britain had become a consumer society and there was plenty of scope for a good salesman, and he appeared to weather it.

A family story about Fred of this time tells that he ran a grocery store with a 'mate.' Perhaps that mid-1940s wedding photo of Fred at that marriage in Bromley is with this business partner. Fred looks rather prosperous there, so maybe the storekeeping paid well for him. As he would become a 'Store Keeper (Motor Trader)' in the record later, this is probably a true story. Every time I look at that photo, I recall Archie Carver, that entrepreneurial, get-rich-quick storekeeper in a well-known, much later fictional book series set across the wars in Fred's very region of England. Of course, he could put anything in the record, which would suit him fine, in keeping with much that I know about him now. My mind could not help racing through the possibilities, as motor trader seemed to me an odd tag for him; what did he know about motor cars? Given his salesman occupation and the way he seemed to get around, he probably had one by now. A year had passed at 26 Carter Drive with an apparently domesticated Fred and Daphne and three children, until I was born on 27 December 1941. This is where Fred stated he was a 'Storekeeper (Motor Trader),' his wartime occupation now.

It would have been a cold winter's day at the height of the blitz on London in WWII in December 1941. Probably those sirens would have been wailing. Anyone knowing the history of that war in Britain would know that was a dark time for people in northern London, probably more so than anywhere else in England, with the threat just across the

Channel. I was born at Oldchurch Road Hospital, Southwest Romford; it used to be a workhouse, built in 1838. A past workhouse for one's entry to the world later was rather prophetic in a way. But something was clearly amiss in their marriage and a separation had taken place. Why was my birth not at home this time not like all the others? Events to follow probably show the reason why. By this time, Daphne had moved out of 26 Carter Drive and we were with her and her grandparents at 72, or maybe it was just us and Daphne in Ipswich in Suffolk. I just do not know.

As I reflected on all that before I came to those dark days for Britain in the aftermath of Dunkirk, I would have thought there might have been some talk between them of the future, now they were married with children arriving. Did he ever ask himself, with his big Australian family in mind, if it was time to go home? In England, there was talk and worry then about invasion and what might happen if it did come. I know my mother must have been thinking about that, and she was worried about the Jewish matter at the time. One memory I can recall about her 'England' is her telling me something while I was on holiday with her one time from Swan. The Jewish matter was why I wasn't circumcised! But Fred, as I am pretty certain now, kept quiet with Daphne about his Australian family connections. I could never come to grips with the relationship between Daphne and her parents during this period, as the story of what happened to us soon after this time unfolded from those files. Before I was born, it looked very much like a family coming together for the first time, all living in the same street; I believe I know now why Carter Drive would loom large in my memory of these times as a result. But this marriage was doomed to fail like the first.

From what I could learn about Fred and Daphne later, it seemed to me they had little in common. Fred, as usual, seemed to have his own plans. If I believe what Daphne wrote in a letter in August 1949, she had separated from Fred from some time in 1941. So their marriage the year before with three children already seems a paradox. It makes me wonder, did Fred decide to marry her so he could have some hold on the first three children? I see in my file that my progeny might have come into question during Daphne's divorce proceedings, according to a Mrs Jones from the Anglican Church who would appear later in our lives. There really is no doubt though that Fred was my father.

Although both parents are shown on my birth certificate as still living at 26 Carter Drive, Fred's separation from Daphne had taken place by my birth, and was the reason I believe now my birth wasn't at home. Later letters from our grandparents say that they brought us up from childhood but when that started is not clear – but precise dates do not matter really. It is suffice to say that all the correspondence indicates that after my birth we were with our grandparents at 72 Carter Drive and Fred was up the road at 26. What Daphne was doing and where she was living I just do not know. As for Fred, during the war years and soon after, I believe he was mainly in business with the partner I referred to earlier. Given his past occupations, I am certain he kept up the salesman role. His divorce from Daphne wasn't finalised until well after the war and they lived apart from my birth on.

Some correspondence written later about us and by others and alluded to in one of Fred's accounts at the time refers to an event involving our care and alleged mistreatment during these war years. This suggests Fred was maintaining some interest in us throughout the war. A mention is made of a case before the Romford courts accusing Daphne of neglect of her children. But I found no record of this. I do not remember Fred at all from that time, only our grandparents. In fact, I have no memory of him at all in England. I remember little of that period of my life anyway. Although I do remember the school we went to, Clock House Lane, and Semolina pudding and sliding on ice in the schoolyard. Bomb craters in Carter Drive are strong memories. And the two-story corner house where we lived with our grandparents. The school is still there and so is our grandparents' house. There is a particular siren sound associated with that period that I, and surely anybody living in London during those times, still recognise. When I hear that same sound now it is like a message from that time saying – remember?

I have little memory of Daphne from that time either. I believe she had gone away, coming back to visit us occasionally. After the war I have a memory of walking down country lanes with her and going to places like Havering

Green, just north of Romford, staying in a house, and a derelict bus I could see outside my window. A moonlight walk with a water tower following us, illuminated by the full moon, frightened me then and haunted me as a youth even at Swan. I know where that water tower is now, as I have seen it since. Driving past it not so long ago, when working in that part of England, I recognised it instantly as if it were engraved in my memory. It was now though, that Daphne was to take charge of us – well, our future anyway – and Fred was not to be part of what she had in mind.

14

ENGLAND TO AUSTRALIA

In the period shortly after the war, I believe now my mother Daphne was not living with her parents and was quite poor. She was also set on a course to remove Fred from our lives as well as divorce him. The four of us were in the care of our grandparents while she earned a living elsewhere, mainly working in hospitals. Only a scant and faint memory of that time at 72 Carter Drive, Romford, stays with me; anything else was probably obliterated by what would follow next in my life. What remains of it is a memory of a straight and dark staircase leading to our upstairs bedroom; which I must have shared, at least with my brothers. My toys were a clockwork railway engine in LNER livery (used for passenger locomotives 1923–1941) and a red-and-white hulled tugboat, which I distinctly remember floating in the bath, not knowing it was just a model made of papier maché! I hung on to it in its forlorn state. Boats would figure in my life soon, and later on, very much so. We would take no toys with us when we left our grandparents' place; just a simple regulation cardboard suitcase with a change of clothes. Although our mother took us away for day trips after the war, all I really remember is that house, which still exists, much updated, like the Clock House Lane primary school I briefly attended.

From our grandparents' letters that came to light after so many years, filed away by the authorities who took us in care, I know they loved us very much. After we left, they would never see us again. I do not blame the church or the authorities for holding those letters after we left care. Nor do I blame the authorities for me not knowing our grandparents' role in our lives and for keeping certain information filed away for so long. I cannot read their letters now without great sorrow and a sense of loss. Sadly, I have little memory of them to support that feeling. They lost their family and became estranged from their only daughter because of what happened. But what did happen to us? Put simply, we were placed under the responsibility and care of the Anglican Church Empire Settlement Scheme at some time in early 1949, when I was seven. The State Government of Western Australia, where we were headed, would 'own us'; there is no more apt expression than the latter. It was the Anglican Church who would run our lives until we had to leave, when we 'came of a certain age,' so to speak.

The records show my mother had it in her mind for us to immigrate to Australia as a family soon after she separated from Fred. Whether it was Fred who put that thought there, with any mention he might have made of his origins, I cannot know, but it is doubtful, given that he appeared not to care what happened to us. The publicity given to the Australian policy of 'populate or perish' was widely spread, so likely that provided the idea, but it does not matter to me now. How the Anglican Church settlement organisation became involved is another question that needed to be answered in my mind. I still do not have all the answers and probably never will. But how did it happen that we were whisked away by our mother in what appeared a clandestine way, in cahoots with the authorities in the Anglican Church and the Australian Government? Harsh words, but Australia House on The Strand and a certain Mrs Jones must have known the role of our grandparents; it was on the application form! But good English stock could not be refused by Australia during those troubling times not long after the war.

In November 1948, Daphne set the wheels in motion to make a new future for herself and her children without Fred. She had been living apart from Fred, where, I could not establish, from at least since I was born. This would make some later remarks by persons involved in our future welfare about who I, in particular, belonged to, quite interesting reading. Fred appeared to ignore this fact later on. At this time, although clearly separated, they were still married, and no divorce proceedings had yet been set in motion. From the record, she made the first visit to Australia House without us. I feel certain this was so, as the only medical reports for us were much later. At first, it seemed, we were all going to emigrate together with our mother to South Australia, as all our names are together on the Australia House immigration application form. This was a family migration form which mentions only her, us, and her parents.

She lists her place of work as part time at Oldchurch

Hospital, Romford, a place of significance for me later, and her occupation as a domestic. She stated she would arrive in Australia with a capital of £10. But that all changed, almost as if it happened on the day. Our names are shown crossed out, with no explanation other than a note across the bottom of the form. This notation indicates the church had been in regular contact with Australia House as a matter of policy, in the form of the Church of England advisory council of Empire Settlement. The note recommends us as 'suitable settler children.'

Interestingly, there is no medical report with this application form, which indicates to me it was aborted for some reason. So, did our mother have a prior dialogue with the Anglican Church about migration, or did Australia House point her in that direction because of her straitened circumstances? The Australian policy of populate or perish might indicate so, and I tend to believe this was the case. Anyway, a new Child Migration form for each of us was raised early the next year. I can find no explanation for why the 1948 earlier attempt was aborted, other than that she was sincere but realized she could not go ahead due to the cost. Or was it fear of Fred finding out, as surely custody of us would have been questioned when such a step was undertaken? It was at this stage that she followed the advice from Australia House and started a dialogue with the Anglican Church, which would seal our fate.

On this original attempt, I also wondered if it was the £10 per person, or the £5 for a child, that she would have been responsible for that made her seek some other help after that first visit. Fifty pounds was a lot of money then, about $5,000 today, and she would not have such an amount at hand, as well as money to live on after arrival. That extra £10 capital she said she had wouldn't go very far with four children and no husband in Adelaide or Fremantle, where we would have eventually ended up. Daphne is still shown as a hospital domestic on the individual forms that she signed for us at the time. She could not have asked her parents for the money, obviously, as the fact that they knew nothing of her plans is clear from what they later wrote to Swan, asking where we were. Yet, curiously, their names as well as Fred's appear on the later forms that sealed our destiny. The appearance of those names and their apparent role in our care did not appear to raise any flags at Australia House.

This is where the church settlement organisation came into play; their physical presence in the process is evident. The letters from the Swan Homes archive include the early correspondence about what happened at the English end; they show that Daphne was in close consultation with the principals who orchestrated the Church of England Child Migration scheme. One of them was a Mrs Enid Jones, the secretary of the Churches' Advisory Council on the Empire Settlement Scheme in London. Mrs Jones would get an MBE, but if it was for the same work, I do not know. The church was a party to the child migration scheme, as is so well-known and written about now, its merits and failures tested to the extreme. A mysterious Mrs Anderson, also from the church, is referred to in our later grandparent's letters in a derogatory way, as if she interfered. From the accounts on record though, it was Mrs Jones who seemed to take charge of Daphne's plans at this stage.

In March 1949, we all went to Australia House. Apparently Daphne took us all on a day trip to London, which might have included the Tower of London, quite a diversion to take one's mind off the real purpose. The Tower is only about twenty minutes away from Australia House by tube. Was it disguised as a trip to the Tower for a child of seven, who had seen little but terraced houses in Romford? I can still remember such a visit as a child. I was at the age to appreciate the crown jewels, the gory parts of it, the chopping block and the axes, and when I read a book about it now, I can feel as if I had been there. I remember my mother with me, so is that the memory of that particular momentous visit to The Strand?

I believe it was that occasion that would fit with any excited account we might relate to our grandparents later, any visit to The Strand buried by it. This was when our individual Australia House immigration forms were raised, and we are shown as still in the custody of our grandparents, but the entity responsible for our welfare and the cost of our travel is shown as the Anglican Church's child migration office. Mrs Jones signed our forms, although they were obviously completed by our mother, as it is the same handwriting as in 1948. When we arrived, we would all become wards of the State, and it would all come as a surprise for our grandparents, as I now know. Did our mother realise what that all really meant? – I only can wonder now. Daphne took our Australia House medical forms back to Romford, as they showed we were checked by a local doctor.

The doctor's reports showed we were all quite healthy; on our family form in March 1949 there is a poignant handwritten annotation by the doctor – 'good family' – and later, by somebody at Australia House, another indecipherable signature with the annotation 'all fine lively healthy looking children, Mother good average type who hopes to accompany them.' But there was no chance of that happening at that stage! It was a surprise reading, that description of us, working-class children of post-war rationed Londoners. In the early image of the four of us in our grandparent's back garden at Carter Drive, we don't look underfed, so it shows we were well cared for.

All our forms were witnessed by my eldest brother Don's headmaster at his senior school in London Road, signature indecipherable. So, our Clock House Lane primary school might not have known what was happening to at least three of us! How this was concealed from our grandparents, though, is difficult to comprehend. Daphne appeared to be living with them then, according to that first aborted family immigration form, which further raises the question of how she concealed it all. Not long after, by the signature dates, we left Romford by train, a journey I still vaguely remember. It was through London to Southampton docks, not the seaside, as I thought. Although our grandparents might have thought we had gone on a seaside holiday, it's likely our school knew we weren't coming back, if Don's headmaster had told them. We would in fact all end up by the seaside, but in another country!

When I look back at this sequence of events involving Australia House and the church, it is clear to me that in those times, although with good intentions perhaps, the authorities worked closely together, and Daphne's brood fitted their criteria as' good English settler stock.' However, all throughout, I believe it was her aim to give us a better life than what she saw for us in Romford; a life she believed she could not provide there. The first attempt to emigrate as a family is very telling. Did she believe, from the advice given by those two offices that she could have somebody else pay, and just collect her children when she came over? An unanswerable question, but the subsequent execution of our immigration appears to have been awash with collusion and subterfuge by Daphne and those two offices.

There is no doubt that Fred's failure to take responsibility for us was at the core if it. Whether she successfully concealed all of it from her parents and from Fred is difficult to imagine, even though later letters indicate they knew little of her plans. But they did know about the church's role and the medicals beforehand, as they mention a Mrs Anderson in their letters, as I referred to earlier. Perhaps it was the final flight of all of us to Southampton that took them by surprise, as later letters show, and they weren't aware of how far our immigration to Australia had progressed. It does not matter now, of course. But there is also the matter of why the officials at Australia House ignored our father; they had a duty of care, surely, to notify him of events, as they knew about him. And that our grandparents were our guardians; it's there on the forms. Also, Fred surely had a history on file at Australia House, but perhaps the twenty year plus gap kept that hidden.

But things moved pretty fast then, as not long after my visit to the Tower and Australia House, the separation of us from our father, mother, and grandparents were added to Fred's from his first wife Grace, and from Daphne. What a disaster to add to the others Fred had been responsible for earlier, though not entirely his fault this time! We were heading for Fremantle, Western Australia, to this so-called land of 'Oranges and Sunshine'; in fact there would be oranges where we finally ended up. I wonder now if Daphne had, after all, found out about Fred's close relatives in eastern Australia and wanted us as far away from them as possible, so crossed South Australia off her list; his family were also living in Adelaide. But it is unlikely she knew that. She did not have any choice in where we were sent; that choice now belonged to the Anglican Church and the Australian Immigration Department.

We left Southampton on May 3 1949 on the S.S. *Asturias* – a ship's name that I know now had greater significance than I could ever have imagined. There were twenty-four children in our little group, according to the report in the *West Australian* on May 4. There were actually only twenty-one, and we didn't lose anybody on the way, so I suspect one little family group didn't make it. In our group, there were children from six families. Apart from two singles and a double and us four, there were families of three, four and six children. So as for our grandparents, some big holes were left in some other carers' or parents' hearts in England. It is reported we were escorted by a Miss Jean Taylor, an Australian schoolteacher, and our ages ranged from four to fourteen. I was in the middle somewhere, and although aged seven, the passenger record shows me as six years old. With Fred's disregard of his age, he might have laughed at that error if he had read about it later. The newspaper said we were headed for a place called Swan Homes; I will just call it Swan. I would later find out quite a lot about Swan Homes would appear in the press, as immigration was news then, but it also wasn't only that.

Swan was one of a number of Anglican institutions from all over Australia that cared for orphans and children whose parents could not care from them for whatever reason. It began in 1868 as a cluster of buildings on the banks of the Swan River just north of Midland Junction at a place called Middle Swan. It was rural and amongst vineyards when I was there. It was and still is an idyllic spot for such a home, having retained its isolation today. Swan had a long history as a Boys' Home. Girls came much later from a Perth Anglican Home, but long before we arrived. We were about to join another three hundred or so boys and girls all in the same boat. But we didn't end up at Swan at the start. We went to a place called Sawseaside, or to me, just Coogee. This was part of the Swan Homes. Anyway, I and everybody else involved didn't know it then, except Fred. We had come home in a way, to join Fred's close family living in Australia, a fact Daphne appeared not to know anything about. But it didn't make any difference, as despite my father's Australian origins, we were still considered Poms.

15

SAWSEASIDE

This now becomes a story about my life in the care of Swan Homes from mid 1949 to the end of 1957. It may seem a short time taken as part of a normal length of one's life, but it was the impressionable years of my youth and made me what I came to be. There are stories written today about children who grew up at such places and at such a formative time without parents. I won't add to them with a litany of suffering that some obviously went through. I can recall visiting other similar homes to Swan in my time there, where the care was badly wanting compared to ours. I will stick to Swan and its Sawseaside home as I recount how I stumbled through the necessarily self-taught rules for a happy and mostly conflict-free life with all the other boys and girls without fathers or mothers to guide them. At Swan in my time, there were over two hundred of us, offering plenty of opportunities to keep below the radar. One could liken it to playing to 'street' rules all the time.

I have always thought we were some of the lucky ones. That is not to say bad things did not happen – for some migrant children it was a grim and lonely life and we saw the former on occasions. That my experience was not exactly the same does not mean it did not affect what we became – the lack of parents at that key part of our lives made us different. That it made us different than others from a 'normal' home upbringing I believe to be true to this very day. I don't think the later experience of life changes that to any great degree – you take it to your grave.

We arrived in Fremantle on 28 May 1949. I remember parts of the sea voyage, a concert, and dressing up as Robin Hood in an outfit of green crepe paper than soon fell apart. I wore glasses then, round lenses, National Health issue, with the left eye covered with plaster to correct astigmatism in my right. They did not arrive in Fremantle with me, and so that was the end of that, and my vision defect would remain unnoticed at Swan and ignored by the military when I signed up, until a day on a rifle range much later, when a recruitment sergeant would take notice. It was late afternoon, tea-time in England, or Tiffin as Fred might have liked to call it. We berthed at P Shed, where all migrant ships disembarked, the hopefuls and those like us; the weather was mild, and might have felt like an English summer, even though winter was approaching. I can still recall the atmosphere of it all, the press of bodies in the port arrival hall. That strong smell of tarred rope is guaranteed to bring it all back. The excited chattering of children, as if they had arrived at a holiday location. But there were no holiday brochures handed out about places like Coogee or Swan or the others.

The journey to the home was in a blue and white bus that would later also take us to and from school. The smell of salt air mingled with that of pine trees, and tea-tree comes back to me now. It was late in the day, in the autumn twilight, but not at all like an English one with supper and bed. I remember it was still light when we got to Coogee. We woke up that first day to the strangest sights and smell of salt air, like on the *Asturias*. And there were the flies of course, never before so many. The cause was an abattoir, the Anchorage, with holding paddocks nearby, and sheep in numbers such as I had never seen. That was where, I soon discovered, we got our meat, mostly offal like liver and kidney and oxtail, with an occasional joint or scraggy end. The meat workers at the Anchorage would regularly appear with supplementary gifts for the Coogee home, so we were not forgotten by the outside world.

Coogee, where the Sawseaside Home was located, is less than ten kilometres south of Fremantle. The home was once called the Coogee Hotel, built and operated by the Palmer family of Cockburn, the name for the general area. It became a beachside holiday hotel and was quite successful in its time. Its licence was taken away in later years, due to the local government's view that there was one too many in the district. It sat vacant until the church bought it around 1930, but they did not occupy it permanently until the first child migrants were taken in. Before that it was a holiday home for the Swan kids at Christmas time. Sawseaside was the Anglican Church's official name for the home, after a church dignitary, William A. Saw, a member of the Anglican Church committee that purchased the hotel. I hesitate to call it an orphanage, it is such an emotive term, but there were some there and at Swan later who had no mum and dad like I had. At that stage, I cannot recall missing either of my parents; it was all an adventure for me. We were the third intake of child migrants for the main Anglican-run home called Swan.

Swan had commenced taking migrant children in 1947, and they were first sent to Coogee, which was used as a starting place, I believe, for the English kids to acclimatise, keeping us separated from the main home at Swan until we were ready to mix with the Aussie kids. There were a handful of local children already at Coogee, but I don't remember them being any different from us. Peterkin, the 'Boss' who ran it all, did not write about it in that way in his memoir about his time at Swan. He only referred to the place as a holiday home for Swan kids. In his daily diary, he mentions the migrant children often. But in time, there was a government push not to mix migrant children with the Aussie kids immediately, so maybe Peterkin was ahead of his time. It did ease us into the dramatic changes to our life, coming from a still rationed and battered Britain to the Australian seaside. I had no memory of going to the seaside before Coogee, so it was all very new to me.

I had never before seen sand so white and such a blue sky. I would find out that Fremantle and most of Perth's western approaches were built on sand; sand was everywhere, and especially at Coogee. Wherever we dug a hole, as kids always do, the sand was ready to bury us as we tunnelled. Later, I would begin to wonder how all the buildings stood up there.

Compared with the streets of Romford, it must have seemed like paradise to someone like me. And it was close to the sea, a reckless run across a tarred main coastal road, past a shop selling sweets and ice-creams, a stretch of grass that seemed always neatly mown, some caravans scattered here and there, a railway track that seemed to be unused. Then, high sand hills, white sand, so white, fine, and squeaky the sand was, and then the sea. The name Sawseaside was most apt, I see now.

When it became a children's home it was run from its start by a Bruce and Ellen Logan. They had a daughter Lorraine, old enough to be called an adult, also on the staff, and a son who would visit occasionally. Mr Logan was the cook and Matron Logan the Grandma to us all. They had been dairy farming people down south Collie way, but as the story goes, walked off their farm in the late 1930s – like so many from that time, I assume, because of the Great Depression. What little I now know of farmer is that they are usually caring people, and this was true of the Logans. Fortunately for us, after their losses, they chose to look after children, and they were good at it. Matron Logan kept a daily diary; likely it was an official requirement, as did Peterkin too. I now have all the pages that refer to us. I wish I had the rest, but that was not allowed for privacy reasons, which is moot, given how long ago it was and all the brouhaha and public enquiries since then. But I am thankful for small mercies, and to the church for releasing them. Without them, there would have had to be much more invention, due to fading memories.

Apart from those few local kids, it was mainly us migrants

who made up the tally of thirty or so. As the migrants came yearly, the number would fluctuate as the children progressed to Swan; we were deemed assimilated in around a year! To make it into the Coogee Orphanage, as it was always called by the Fremantle press, extra facilities like boys' and girls' dormitories and a larger laundry were built. Probably the rooms had been knocked down to make our dorms and the dining hall where we also had picture shows. On the south side, they built an outhouse or play shed that I cannot remember using as such. But it was important to me, as I found underneath it, on a street facing south, a refuge at times. It was where I used to go and hide and dream of things I wished to be and other daring adventures; there weren't many private places at Coogee. It was not a big place and the grounds were small, compared to Swan.

Fred's visits to see us began at Coogee and were regular, as he operated to a sailing schedule. He had gone to sea on the Australia run. By this time he definitely knew what had happened to us. As to what Fred knew or thought about us leaving Romford and in such an abrupt way, I will never really know. But from what I know about him now, he would have been furious, I believe. I venture Fred knew what vessel we were on before we left, and he knew where we were and what had happened with the Anglican Church and us. This is apparent from his letters to Peterkin which began at this time. The name of our ship may have made him smile when he found out, as of course he had travelled on a same-named ship before. Despite being an obvious absence in our life in England, even though he lived just down the road, I do think now that he cared, as we will see. Perhaps this event of our departure for Australia was the turning point in his life! He would make a lasting impression on me during these visits to us at Sawseaside.

When he first appeared at Coogee, he was a deck steward on the *Moreton Bay* and his first sailing was from the port of London on March 31 1949. So he had left before we did, which I found interesting, given he was not involved in our immigration. In one of her letters Daphne scornfully called it a tramp steamer, so she knew where he was, but did she know he was heading for Australia? On the crew list he stated he was forty-nine, and born in Singapore, and a British Subject. With no regard for his Australian parentage, this erroneous information seemed a denial of his roots that was a feature of his early life in England. He knew his family lived in Melbourne but appeared to maintain this idea that he was English on the crew list, even at this late stage in his life, when clearly he was returning to the land of his family and where he grew up.

When Fred arrived in Fremantle on June 16 1949, he had already arranged to see us. He did that by cable from Melbourne to Peterkin, underlining my belief that he knew where we were, and who was in charge, and in what I now know was a typical Fred move, putting his 'stamp' on the process. His visit is logged in Matron Logan's diary a little over two weeks after our arrival. So he came hot on our heels, one could say. As this was a Thursday, we might have missed school that day, but I cannot remember what we actually did. Matron records he 'spoke very highly of the home after he had inspected it and thanked us for the welcome and treatment given the children.' So, this was some sort of inspection, which, I would learn, was typical of his nature. He came that first time with a Mr Robertson, who was the representative in Perth for the Anglican Church Empire Settlement Scheme. You could say Fred was not only making his presence known in the flesh, but making some sort of claim on us. When I look back now, I think he had made up his mind that he had some responsibility for our fate, and was why he appeared so early. Perhaps he was making sure everybody who mattered knew who he was.

So, in spite of Mrs Jones's disparaging remarks about his character, which I found in the record of what the English court said about custody in Daphne's divorce proceedings, Fred was making his presence felt very early in our new life. It didn't matter now; we were a world away from Mrs Jones and belonged to somebody else, the State. Also, it is apparent from the diary that we did not go anywhere with him on this first occasion; this first visit I cannot remember but clearly it took place. On the later visits I do remember, he would take us to South Fremantle and the Esplanade. A rare family studio photograph from then shows a smiling Fred with what you could say was a fatherly air, with us all 'dressed up'. From that time, I can only remember him in his 'whites.' He must have had 'civvies' of course, but in these Coogee visits I mainly remember him in white.

Also, he wore a peaked white cap emblazoned with some sort of badge, likely the merchant line insignia. I now believe that peaked officer's cap might have been an affectation. That type of cap was only issued to officers or petty officers of the Merchant Marine or British Navy. I would say the cap was a harmless remnant of that persona he had created in England for himself.

While we were at Coogee, Fred would visit us four times as his ship passed through Fremantle; the last time was in September 1950. Early on in this time, he would use the term inspecting Coogee and Swan in one of his letters to Peterkin. When I recall that sort of remark, after reading the diary entry of his visits, and what I know now, I get the impression that this was Fred the Captain speaking. He was only a ship's steward, but you might have thought him something else. He bought us clothes one time, but I have no memory of what they were. They are described as 'a new suit for each child' according to Matron, but I found no photos of me dressed so, except for that one photo with Fred of us all dressed the same. We were soon back wearing our home clobber, which is all I remember wearing: sandals for going out, no shoes, and hand-me-down shorts and shirt. But they were always clean and the jumpers well darned. On one occasion, he brought 'flowers for the ladies,' and on another, two pounds of Orange Peko tea, which was a big hit, and was shared with Mrs Peterkin, who had been visiting from Swan. Matron's comments on him in the diary suggest he made a fuss of them. I see this as him in character again, a ladies' man, maintaining his persona as a man of means, gentleman and man of the world, as was one of his aspiration I believe now.

Soon after our arrival at Coogee, the records show an extensive file of correspondence about our well-being. Letters are from our parents, grandparents, and some church luminaries in the child migration re-settlement business, not just Anglican – all addressed to Peterkin. At the same time, Fred and Daphne were having a war in court in Colchester in the divorce proceedings, and commenting on who was saying bad things about Swan to our grandparents. All of this reached the desk of Peterkin and ultimately, Matron Logan. The correspondence doesn't readily show who was causing all the fuss back in England. Daphne claimed Fred was making remarks like we were 'ill-clad, thin and a bundle of nerves' and that Fred said this to our grandparents. Peterkin thought Daphne was the troublemaker, but I found nothing to support either, and it is unclear who was to blame.

Mrs Jones got involved and wrote a letter not complimentary about Fred to an administrator of their settlement scheme. She said she had had a talk with him and got promises he would not interfere, presumably in our 'abduction' by our mother, which is probably as he saw it. Where and how Mrs Jones met Fred is not clear, but it shows she was actively involved with both. Who was interfering in what is difficult to fathom. But it was all over for Fred and Daphne now, as we belonged to the State, albeit in the care of the Anglican Church. But was is clear from Daphne's letters, is that she thought she still had custody of us after her decree nisi. In the divorce hearing reported on by Mrs Jones, the main feature seemed to be what children Daphne had custody of after the divorce and making that statement on my parentage I referred to earlier. If we had remained at our grandparents, surely custody would have been by them via Daphne? But it didn't matter now.

We were thousands of miles away in the care of Matron, Peterkin, and the State, so any ruling by the divorce court was irrelevant anyway. Daphne was very wrong about any outcome in her favour, if she thought that she could take us back as soon as she arrived. Whether she really thought that I will never know! The Romford court divorce records I could not find, but it is likely that any custody dispute would have been in her favour, from what the church wrote about it. And, the Anglican settlement scheme had a provision for cases like ours; parent(s) in desperate circumstances, with children who were from a broken home but not in care, could take back the children as soon as they were able to after arriving in Australia. That was easier said than done, particularly for the mother, as we will see, because in reality, it was the State who owned us, not the church, who were only guarantors for our upkeep; the State set the bar very high for any parent, as Daphne would find out. I believe now she had every intention to try; why else would she have migrated from England, and so quickly?

According to Matron's diary, at the end of June 1949, we

each received a letter from our grandparents. The gist of these very first letters show that our grandparents thought we had gone on a holiday on the Sussex coast. Such an extraordinary deception by our mother is difficult to believe; but one cannot make a judgement now about who was deceiving who, for the truth is lost to history. These letters came as enclosures written by our grandmother to each of us, with a short letter to Matron from our grandfather, Leonard Bellamy, from their home at 72 Carter Drive, where we had lived without our mother for what looks like most of our childhood. This was confirmation that that was where we had been living whilst all these preparations for our departure were going on, and it is the only place I remember as a home in England. What they show is a deepening estrangement between Daphne and her parents at this time. I do not know if they ever reconnected; sadly, there was little time left for her to do so, as it would transpire. What was also apparent is that Fred was closer to our grandparents, to the extent that it appeared to overshadow any relationship between them and Daphne by this time. I can only speculate how this came about. Did Fred work his charm on them? What is clear is that it looked like our mother was estranged from her parents even before we were shipped out to Australia. It is also clear, from this first letter to each of us, that it was Fred who told them where we were.

How is it that I did not know then, and even in the immediate years, how much they cared, and that they did not know about Swan and the church's role? Mrs Logan said in the diary that we each sat down and wrote a reply, but I have no memory of that. A photocopy of my grandfather's letter survives, but not ours; it was sent to Swan by Matron, who fortunately, for whatever reason, transcribed each of the letters to us from our grandparents, and photocopies of them in her hand survive. We would never have known our grandparent's story if she hadn't, bless her! The letters written by our grandmother in July 1949 to each of us at Coogee have no place here. But I make an exception for one extract, that to my eldest brother Donald; as he was the eldest, he was likely the one they knew best of all. His letter is the longest (ours are quite short) and uses the strongest language about Daphne. The words imply that they brought him up from babyhood. Like that letter Fred wrote to the India Office, it is important to know precisely sometimes what people said. So, here is part of it, but I cannot include the most powerful parts. It speaks for itself.

> My Dearest Donald, I never thought the day would come when I should be writing to you all these thousands of miles away. How are you my dear one I hope you are coping well & fit. I am sorry to say your Grandad and myself have been very queer over the shock of finding out where your mother had sent you all. We have not seen her since the day she took you from us and put you on the ship. We are writing to your brothers & dear sister so will you all try & send your Grandad & myself nice long letters all about yourself & life out there. We miss you so my dear boy & pray that we may be spared to see you all again someday. So keep your chin up like we are trying to do ...

Was it for some higher reason, or was it because she wanted to make sure the truth was known about our grandparents' views, that Matron Logan sent the transcriptions in a formal letter to Peterkin? That they survived shows that Peterkin was a stickler for keeping records – or was he making sure the true record was kept for posterity? Clearly, she wanted each of us to retain our original letters and recognised what they might have meant to us. There is a brief note from her to Peterkin appended to that letter. They had probably heard it all before many times over in other cases, but the emotion in that short note, referring to our grandparents' bewilderment, is poignant.

The Logans were fair and kind people, despite the experiences of some others like us in the same situation, and this shows that perhaps they cared beyond what was expected of people like them. I can still conjure up the image and personality of Mrs Logan in my mind and it fits my words. Our grandfather, Leonard, also wrote to Peterkin along similar lines not long afterwards. What would a seven-year-old make of all that, when he seemed to be in a far better place than Romford, going to the beach just across the road, with enough to eat? What I really thought I cannot remember, but I wonder now why not, as I should be able to from that age. It makes me think there is a blockage in my memory, some trick played on my mind, not wanting to reveal more, perhaps. I do not recall reading my letter but when I read the transcript now so many years later, I cannot begin to describe how it makes me feel. I am overwhelmed by emotion and a sense of lost chances and hopes. And not only for me, what about our grandparents?

We would not hear from our grandparents again. After we had all written back to them, as the diary note says we did, there were no more letters from them directly to us; but the correspondence about us between them and Peterkin at Swan continued unabated. They had been our carers from a very young age; that is apparent and not only from the record. But the young heart forgets so easily, and absence doesn't make it grow fonder. Whoever thought of that saying did not know life. Anyway, Fred had already come to see us, bearing us gifts and for our keepers, and would continue to on a regular basis when his ship passed through until we left for Swan. And our mother was on her way but did not arrive until December 1950.

Daphne emigrated under the £10 passage scheme just like us, travelling on the same *Asturias* and arriving in Fremantle on December 18 1950, having left on November 23. So, it was nearly a year-and-a-half before we saw her again. From the passenger list, of the immigrants for Fremantle, just under half were single women, ranging from nurses to domestics like her. A representative demographic of those times I suppose, but how many were following their children? Did she meet anybody on board, I wonder, male or female? Her divorce from Fred was absolute. She was in her early thirties and still an attractive woman. What followed makes me believe that she thrived on companionship. From what I recall, and from anecdotal sources, she was not a shrinking violet, and she could play the piano; she most certainly overshadowed Fred on that score.

Before she left, she had won the custody battle with Fred in the Romford magistrate's court, so she may have had expectations of starting a new life far away from the one she knew. I only have the church's viewpoint on what transpired, and it is obvious they took her side. Mrs Jones's account indicates the church representatives were present during proceedings, and an exchange with the clerk of the courts indicates they might have been pally with the officials, due to their assumed role as our keepers, I might suppose. Mrs Jones's letters also refer to a talk with Fred where she said he promised not to continue harassing Daphne, whom he had allegedly called a drunkard. That they were in a position to make such statements indicates a greater level of participation in Fred and Daphne's affairs than I had expected.

At 72 Carter Drive, Romford on a summer day post war. Me doing my own thing clothes wise? (from Daphne)

SS *Asturias* 1949 with single funnel. She once had two. (Private collection)

English Migrants for Swan Homes, arrival around 1951 with Mrs E. Jones far right. (Courtesy *The West Australian* archive)

Coogee Dining room, me in front row, gazing at the camera.
Taken in the early Swan days, Christmas break.
(Courtesy Perth Anglican Diocese archive)

Sawseaside Home, Coogee. Viewed from rear, facing Southwest with road and bus shelter just visible to right of building. The road ran south from right to left. Sea is just beyond low scrub to right of roof line. Main entrance was road-side. By the time we arrived a raised floor for the veranda had been built along the north wall starting from where the people are standing. (Courtesy Perth Anglican Diocese archive)

Matron Logan at rear of the group, around 1950. Most of us smiling and me in front row second from left. Taken on the north side of the building on the veranda where we slept sometimes in hot weather.
(Courtesy Perth Anglican Diocese archive)

Fred in his 'whites' with us in our 'suit of clothes', Don proudly copying Fred's pocket of pens. Coogee, Fremantle, probably mid 1950. (studio unknown)

The harbour service vessel MV *Wandoo* arriving at Garden Island with rampant Swan kids from a different world! (Courtesy Perth Anglican Diocese archive)

The 1949 Child Migrant group, Swan, around 1951. My oldest brother in the middle row, far right, sister and other brother back row, right. Me in front row, on my own with cheeky grin. (Courtesy Perth Anglican Diocese archive)

Waylen House for the junior boys dormitories as I remember it before the open Gabled Weather portal was erected on the end in view. Wet bed veranda is on left with open shutters. View is from the track that leads to Cornwell House. (Courtesy Perth Anglican Diocese archive)

Waylen House dorm exactly how it was for me. Bed-heads are to the centre; to keep us from waving to each other. (Courtesy Perth Anglican Diocese archive)

The Chevy with Swan kids. Coogee Christmas break for those not sent to someone who cared. This was how we travelled from Swan before the Bluebird. (Courtesy Perth Anglican Diocese archive)

View looking East from Waylen House. The distant tree line marks Jane Brook and the roof of Cornwell House in the distance. The boys garden and kitchen/dining room are to the right of frame. (Courtesy Perth Anglican Diocese archive)

The boys gardens with Huddleston House in background. Inscribed on the back of this photo are the rather enigmatic words; 'Where there's faith there's hope. Where there's gardens M. Cope'. (Courtesy Perth Anglican Diocese archive)

The dining room, kitchens were to the left. Staff would eat on the elevated tables at the far end. This was also where we had Prep. (Courtesy Perth Anglican Diocese archive)

Boys and girls swimming separately, in the Swan River ... look out for the snags! (Courtesy Perth Anglican Diocese archive)

St Marys Swan Sea Scouts in Navy Cutter *Leeuwin*, Naval Base. (Private collection)

St Marys Swan Sea Scouts with Vic Davies, Troop leader, Bassendean. Me on the left. (Private collection)

Swan Mosquito Weights shaping up and that 'punishment gym horse'. (Courtesy Perth Anglican Diocese)

Daphne, me and my sister, at Swan, around 1955. before Daphne lost hope perhaps! (Daphne's collection)

At Swan, in typical Swan clobber – boys barefoot (not as Fred might have liked as with him in Coogee), around 1954. Showing we really were all in the one place more than once. Me on the right without those glasses! (Daphne's collection)

Senior girls tour in Bluebird bus, with my sister far left, rear, 1954. (Courtesy Perth Anglican Diocese).

Ross Peterkin, as I remember him. (Courtesy Perth Anglican Diocese)

16

A COOGEE LIFE

I spent about a year and a half at Coogee. Matron's diary tells who did what and who was sick or who went where, such as to the dentist or the doctor, or at times with people who cared or had local children at Coogee. She mentions local children who would go away for the weekend or on holidays, sometimes taking us migrant children. All the names from our child migrant group of 1949 are there. Matron records other visitors bringing sheet music and some gifts like dolls, and giving dancing lessons to the girls. On Sunday June 12 1949, the diary reads that a Mr and Mrs Yates brought a beautiful doll to give to my sister. So, we began to figure in daily life not long after our arrival. From these notes, with the help of that unreliable memory, I will try to give some idea of what our life was like.

Fred's appearance in the diary on every visit underscores his presence in our lives then. It is clear from all the correspondence between him and Peterkin that he saw himself as the protagonist in our life in terms of family. Peterkin also from what transpired. Throughout the rest of the following year, there was correspondence between Fred, our grandparents, and Peterkin, mostly about what Daphne was planning when she arrived, and from our grandparents' side, the estrangement of Daphne that firm opinions about her became settled in their minds. The words he used suggest that Fred was very concerned about what plans she might have for us when she arrived. At the same time, the storm of words, and accusations about who had said 'bad things' about what was happening to us continued. But for us, it didn't change a thing. We were on our way to becoming Aussies and living in a place that was a far cry from the streets of Romford.

Life went on at this beachside home, which we all now called Coogee rather than that other official name, blissfully unaware of the war of words between Fred, Daphne, our grandparents, with Mrs Jones championing our mothers' cause, and Peterkin at the centre of it all. I did not have to wait for the summer months to truly enjoy living; I have a memory of it always being warm, and soon forgot Romford winters, bricks and concrete, and Clock House Lane School. The beach was the centre of attraction, for me at least. We wore woollen bathers that let sand in in places where it shouldn't be allowed. I will always remember running along the beach to the wreck near the Anchorage Abattoir, getting the offal that had washed down from there between our toes, and throwing it at each other. The wreck was where we swam and pretended we were pirates, always with a hidden fear of the corroding metal ribs like rusty fangs, and wondering what lurked in the dark places.

I know more of that wreck now. She was the *Omeo*, a barque, a rigged iron screw steamer that plied the northwest coast; she had broken her moorings off Cockburn Sound and run aground off Coogee. Her history is well documented; from that account, she earned her keep all around Australia and in the Pacific; but to me she was a playground. It was where the meatworks spilled its guts, seemingly without check; in fact, the record says the outflow pipe was within the wreck. Later reports I found in the press showed that practice was soon to cease. The wreck is still there, but no longer lying on the beach, which is long gone, eroded away by our modern world. I am glad signs of the wreck remain, as it is one of the signposts of my life at Coogee. I can visualise still that high counter stern and proud raking bow and lingering smell of rusting iron; that all long gone now, marked only by a pile.

I remember spending hours hiding in the pine tree that grew on our northern roadside boundary. It had flat fronds like boy-size branches, where we would lie, counting the cars passing by; it was a slow count then. We travelled on that same road to the Beaconsfield Primary school, riding on the blue and yellow bus of the Coogee Spearwood Bus Company. Their buses were small and coach-like, maybe for less than thirty people, and had that distinctive engine out front like a small truck, which I now know as a distinctly American style. They were similar to the country bus we took to Havering with our mother in another time and place. They were Fords, with their rounded friendly mudguards and grinning grills of shiny chrome; their blue and yellow livery was seemingly in harmony with the sand and the sea that was so much part of life at Coogee. We must have wished it would go on forever, but of course, it didn't.

We were destined to leave soon for Swan. When I now read the accounts of others not so lucky, I say thanks, Peterkin, for that idyllic introduction to Australian life!

Of the thirty-odd children at Coogee nobody stands out that made my life different during that time, staff or friend, Matron apart of course. I must have kept a low profile, from the little that is said about me in the diary. I am only mentioned twice for the eighteen months I was there. I'm just shown as being present, nothing exciting. Early in my first year, my black cat arrived; that's what I call it. It was a friend who wasn't real, but was always there when I wanted to be on my own under the shed I mentioned earlier. The other thing that arrived in September 1949 was a playground object, accompanied by much fanfare, as I recall. Matron recorded the event, but I well remember it anyway. It was a gift from the Lumpers, those wharfies. They were represented by a Messrs Booth and Mowday; their names appear in Matron's diary as the benefactors. They had ordered it for the home from Cyclone, a well-known Australian fencing company, whose products appeared everywhere then, mainly as cheap urban and country fencing.

It was something similar to a May pole you dance around with ribbons; you might ask why a well-known Australian company would choose such a device to entertain children – one that resembled something from these English children's past lives, but was so dynamically different. It was a very tall metal pole with large rings on chains you grasped and ran around the pole with. Of course, all similar things seemed high to me then, but this was well up to the veranda roof line of the main building. Even today, the memory of it makes me laugh and cry inside, and I can still hear the tinkling of the chains, like some harbinger of woe. It became a torture wheel, in effect. The bigger kids would get everybody on it and whirl it till somebody was flung off, and so it became a very effective skin-scraper and bruise-maker. I wonder to this day where the idea came from, as I have never seen one since. Whoever conceived such a playground toy then had no knowledge of the behaviour of some children. It soon became wrapped around itself and immobilised; it was finally taken away, as one day it was there, gone the next.

I don't recall any specific chores we had to do on a regular basis, other than going to collect the meat from the abattoir with a wooden handcart, usually three of us, with at least one a big kid. We used to drag it along the railway line that ran along the shoreline between the road and the sand hills. Records show the train from Fremantle to Coogee had been a popular picnic trip well before we arrived. I do remember there being some rails but not crossing them when we went to the beach, for some reason. It was less than half a mile to the abattoir and I don't recall meeting any trains on those journeys. Records show a Coogee railway operating as late as 1950, when it might have closed for passenger traffic. They would have been steam then, and if they ran, how could I forget it?

Life at Coogee was a simple routine and was scheduled around going to school and finding something to amuse oneself outside it. There was really no structure to it all, and as far as I recall we were allowed to roam free, except for going to the beach. There were no gates, and how far we strayed was governed by the call of our bellies, or if someone noticed you missing. It seemed, though, when I look at it now, as if the Coogee orphanage was surrounded by a feeling of 'we will look after you,' not only from the Matron and her staff, but the local populace and a group of people and associations who went out of their way to entertain and keep a friendly eye on us. If you missed out on some group event because you were chasing your own dream, say, when you turned up staff would say, 'Oh! There you are then, we wondered, but here you are now.' Perhaps this was because it was a small place and still looked like a pub.

Less than a year after our time there, a newly arrived migrant brother and sister, only eleven and six, walked off from Coogee and ended up back in Fremantle, wandering around North Wharf where they had arrived, like us. The story ran in the Press that they were looking for their companions who had arrived from England with them, who had all been sent directly to Swan. One wonders what was going through their minds at the time. There are records showing kids missing the bus from our school in Beaconsfield on the highway just south of Fremantle and wandering off and being found and brought back to the home. I cannot imagine it happening today, I hope. Perhaps I am wrong – was city life just safer then?

Parents of the few local children in the home came and

took their child away for a day or the weekend, and at times would take one of us as well, although I have no memory of going for day outings with anybody, and it would have been in the diary if I did. The diary records that my older brother Don spent quite a lot of time away and was involved with a choir, and often stayed with the choir master. My sister and brothers scored a few days away and even went away during school holidays with people, all named in the diary. My brothers got invited to Mrs Farmer's son's birthday party one time. My older brother was sick, home from school, and I was pleased to read he got boils at one time. My sister and Donald are mentioned most of all. Going for treatment once, but mainly staying with friends and doing much more exciting things. Was it just that year gap and being the youngest that made the difference? It was largely down to whether you made friends with these local kids, and I suspect I didn't. A typical diary entry would read: "Mrs Farmer invited David & Allen Evans, John Davies, Ernie Johns," (older boys from our migrant group), and my brothers to her son's "birthday lunch & tea & all had a very jolly time."

The visits by the Lumpers, the wharf workers, were regular. They also took us on picnics, and later, when at Swan, during holidays spent back at Coogee, to Garden Island on the Wandoo, a harbour work boat that looked much like a tug. Images I have found from those times show us scoffing food and soft drink on these outings, roaming the deck and jetty without an adult in sight, and we seem a happy lot.

I remember them well. When we were at Coogee, if no one took us for Christmas school holidays, we were all sent to Swan, as Coogee itself was used by the boys and girls left behind there as a seaside holiday camp. Later, when we got to Swan, I would experience those Christmas camps back at Coogee. Being parked at Swan for Christmas only happened once for meat Coogee, in December 1949. At the end of 1950, we all went there for good.

When Daphne arrived in late December 1950, I imagine I was told, but I am pretty sure I was at Swan by that time. Matron Logan's diary says she visited on December 19 and stayed for the evening. That was actually the day after her arrival, so she didn't waste time, and the diary mentions that my sister was still there. Don had already gone on holiday. My sister would go on holiday with a Mr Booth a couple of days later. Daphne then took up a position at the Mount Hospital in Perth, and started an exchange with Peterkin regarding our welfare. By this time, it was clear from the letters being exchanged between Fred and Peterkin that Fred was worried about what she planned to do and whether he might still have access to us. Fred says, in one letter he wrote on voyage from the *Moreton Bay* in late December, that he had given Mrs Logan some money for Daphne, saying 'I rather think she may be short of cash.' If he did leave money for Daphne, this was uncharacteristic of what I know about his relations with her. He must have given it to Matron back in September, when he last visited Coogee, according to the diary. From what I found about

Fred's behaviour in England before all of this, this generosity was quite extraordinary. Whether Daphne got this money I don't know, as it is not mentioned later.

So, with our parents now both in Perth, albeit Fred only visiting when his ship was in, things shaped up for what seemed a contest for us, and I expect our affection. And so my time at what I called this holiday place, Coogee, came to a close. By now, all sense of family, including sibling ties, was lost to me. I hadn't yet seen my mother, and Fred was just a bearer of gifts so far. I imagine it now to being at school all the time, something like a boarding school life. Later in when in PNG I would send my children to boarding school, not Scotch College that Fred fantasised but one just as good called Brisbane Grammar and its sister school. An image of my son standing solitary, looking at me as we departed one day haunts me still – dragging me back to Coogee, and Swan. I lived, played, ate and slept with my age group all the time, and that pattern prevailed for the rest of my childhood. I have no memory of doing things with my siblings at Coogee, or even later at Swan – they just seemed to disappear from my life. I cannot conjure up a single Coogee incident when we were doing something together, except when Fred appeared.

I am not saying it didn't happen, just that there is no memory of it. Fred taking us to South Fremantle, to the Esplanade, where the gulls matched his white shorts and shirt, remain in my memory as the only time together. I took those memories to Swan, but have no further ones of

Fred until I left there. Even the death of Matron at Coogee in the last year we were there does not seem to register in my memory; the diary says she had a stroke and died in November 1950. By the beginning of the school year in 1951 we were all at Swan, and this was an entirely different place. There is an image taken of our migrant group soon after we arrived at Swan, and it shows me standing quite apart from my siblings with a grin on my face, as if I had just ducked in for the photo shot at the last minute. It more or less affirms my solitary nature when I left Coogee, and sets the scene for what was to follow.

17

SWAN HOMES

I can stand on a certain spot near where I first arrived so many years ago and it doesn't seem to have changed much at all. There is a statue of children near the main building, more or less in front of the back entrance to Waylen House. They are lifelike but anonymous figures, commemorating the young lives that passed through its many corridors, climbed its stairs and slept in its dormitories and on its verandas; each domain was based on age, except for one veranda. This statue is similar to the one at Fremantle Port, near where we arrived, and that marks that child migration program that changed so many young lives – older ones too of course. Back at that spot, looking northward, there are the headwaters of the eastern reaches of a dark brown Swan River swirling around those scary, slippery snags. I bet they are still there along the banks, where we dived in from a wooden landing place without a care.

It all looks just the same today, although our river swimming place has gone. Closing my eyes, I hear shouts, noisy splashes, cheeky calls and laughter; yes, there was laughter as well as tears. I can still imagine the mulberry tree in the middle of the paddock that we ran past and raided on the way to and from the river; it's gone now. With red fingers from sweet berries, we picked its leaves that fed the silkworms, one of the hobbies we took on, but what for end, I cannot say, as all I remember is squashing the finished cocoons to see what was inside. Looking to the right is the church of St Marys, and behind that, Jane Brook branches off southward and sets another boundary we were not supposed to cross, but which provided another playground in the dry.

The church graveyard, with its resident and possessive magpies, whose song always rang out as if to remind us what country we were in. Settler graves, alongside the new ones that were dug by the older boys in my time; I can picture a boy digging now. I can also picture lines of boys and girls marching to Sunday church, two by two, boys first, then the girls, well-spaced of course; there was no mixing of the sexes allowed at Swan at any time, but that did not stop it happening, of course. This was the only time we saw the girls outside dinner time and any other formal or special arrangement. Then, to the right of my St Marys, that squat and still unchanged building with the red-brick-tiled roof, the place where some of the boys cut and turned wood – a trades building, built by barefoot, hatless boys lumping rafters and laying bricks during the last war. It had other uses, where those who had fallen behind in their studies 'crammed' in the early morning with the Boss, and it was the place where we boxed till we dropped in a boxing ring permanently set up and often used.

That statue is in front of Stanton House, which was the house for smaller boys; at right angles to it, two-storeyed

Waylen House had that same façade. This is where the main part of the home for the bigger boys began, and Peterkin lived down one end with his enigmatic family, his children always smartly dressed in private school uniforms, but we rarely saw them. His sons' school, I would soon learn, was where my brothers would end up, courtesy of Fred. The rest of Waylen was the younger boys' dormitories, with staff accommodation, library, sickbay, and offices in the middle part. It is easy for me to imagine how it all was then; the buildings have hardly changed, although they are somewhat run down, looking at an uncertain future, their original purpose long discarded.

The Boss of Swan, as I have mentioned, was Roy Peterkin. Looking back, I believe he was an honourable man, dedicated to his task of building the character of the children in his care. The memoir he wrote about the part of his life at Swan reinforces that. He may seem harsh at times in this story, but that is because of how it is told, and it must be taken in the context of the times. And, of course, it is written from the memories of a child. To his descendants, I offer only honour and respect for the memory of the man who gave much of his life to helping those less fortunate than others. His memoir helped me, in many ways, to write this part. And so, it is another tribute to him, in a way. Also, I think Peterkin respected Fred and what he tried to do for us along the way. But I also think Fred had his measure, and might have fooled him somewhat as to what he was really like as a person and where he came from … presenting himself as something other than a ship's steward. I now know Fred met Peterkin a number of times, from the record. It might have been about men being the boss, as was the paradigm of that time, but perhaps he saw something in Fred that many others hadn't. Fred would give more us than Daphne in the end, but maybe that was his conscience working, in the end!

Swan didn't only take children from England through the Australian government sponsored child migration scheme. That was a supplement to its main purpose, which had been long established. They took local children from disadvantaged homes; one of these would become my best friend. They were children much like me, with parents at war, as if two world wars weren't enough. Much has been written, and many formal enquiries and rulings made about that child migration scheme. Compared to some stories of child migration, Western Australia and Swan were lucky choices for us, although I suspect now that Daphne did not make these choices. Despite the publicity and desperate accounts of obvious maltreatment in places similar to Swan, I have taken little notice of the enquiries, and paid no attention to the findings and rulings they made. I have never expected an apology from anyone for what happened to me. This is not because I did not see it or feel it – I saw much of it – but it did not affect me in a way that I saw needed any form of retribution or repayment later in my life.

What is important to know about this migration scheme is that all such migrant children became wards of the State. Moreover, the State set the bar very high for their return to those who let them go. So, it is disingenuous to just blame the institutions; the State was equally accountable for both migrant and local children. In the early period of the scheme, the children were sent to Australia to become farmers and domestics, according to the experts who wrote the rules for how those chosen were managed and trained. One only has to ask about the socio-economic level they came from to find the answer why. So this 'little army,' or potential workforce for the farmers and householders of Australia, was formed, and characters moulded in this way. But there would be those amongst them who would become engineers, architects, writers and soldiers, and much more. But that was, of course, beyond the expectations of those who raised them.

So, although the Anglican Church owned and ran Swan, the sometimes heavy hand of the State was present in all that happened to those in the church's care. Letters about my mother clearly show this to be so. The State paid the church a weekly subsidy to keep us. So they rightly had an interest in what happened to us. My subsidy started off at eight shillings and nine pence per week; it was paid until we were sent off to work at sixteen, deemed members of society and made independent. When I left, my subsidy had risen to twenty-two shillings and three pence a week. I knew nothing about that subsidy then; the only finance that passed temporarily through my hands was my Commonwealth Bank Savings book, a government–bank sponsored scheme then for all school children. It started with two shillings, recorded in the book given to me at Beaconsfield Primary when I was at Coogee. That amount crept up to one pound one shilling by March 1951 and then stayed stubbornly at that, until I left without it. Was Fred responsible for those seemingly random deposits I see on the first page? That bank book was passed on to Swan by the State, and survived to be handed to me with copies of my files and those diaries from the Anglican Diocese archives that are now kept at Swan some seventy years later.

Children left high school at sixteen and were placed by the institution into various menial or trade occupations, unless the parent could afford otherwise of course. So, regardless of their desires and sometimes obvious talents, or what they or their parents had in mind, in reality, they had no decision-making power in their life throughout their stay in care or at the end of it. I have no memory of dreaming of a future that would start in uniform. Some were luckier than others and went to higher places if sponsored; Fred made sure that my older brothers got the further education they deserved and were capable of. As for me, I got that Army 'scholarship' and as I said in my opening words, my sister had to make do with what she had when she also left at sixteen.

18

A SWAN ARRIVAL

Matron's last entry about me at Coogee says I had just returned from Swan in early 1950 with another small group of us, after spending some weeks there during the Christmas break. We had to make room at Coogee for the Swan kids left behind for Xmas. That was how it worked then. She also records we had visited Swan with Fred on one of his 'inspections' as I like to call them now, but I have no memory of that. It doesn't appear in Peterkin's diary about me, but Matron was usually right, from what I've seen of the records. I do remember our arrival at Swan – well, our waking up there, knowing we weren't going back to the seaside. I believe that is why this memory is strong. We slept in the same place as we might have done on that earlier Xmas visit. And this time, we awoke to a place that was alive, not more or less deserted. It is a strong memory, but reconstructed with some imagination!

We had arrived late in the day, and the next morning I was woken by the sound of bird calls mixed with voices. They were sharp and cocky, full of slang words, and spoken in a now familiar drawl, but were different in a way. The calls of the birds were new to me. I only remembered the calls of gulls and crows at Coogee. And when I woke, I still had that smell of the sea in my nostrils, the feeling of sand between my toes, and that dryness of the skin that comes from regular swimming in the sea followed by a cold shower. I would always love the sea, and it would become part of my life much later. But the sea was a long way away from Swan. There were crows here too, of course, but this bird sound was new, and the callers controlled the skies here.

That bird sound I heard was the Australian magpie, of course, a birdsong I would take to my heart in time, its morning 'wake up now' warble unmistakable, and always welcome. More often than ever now, when I hear them in the morning, I always think of that place by the Swan River. The other thing I would find is that there wouldn't be any of that white sand to get between my toes; this was the land of clay and gravel, as I would soon find out. It was goodbye Sawseaside holiday home Coogee, hello Swan, a place for around two hundred, mainly local, homeless boys and around a hundred girls.

On that morning, I can still remember one loud voice saying, 'the Pommy kids are here!' My arrival in Australia was confirmed yet again, but in another very different place. These voices, although loud and harsh, were slow and used words I had not heard before, but they did not frighten me. We had been a year-and-a-half at Coogee and had gone to School in Beaconsfield for that time with over a hundred local kids. So, I had heard voices like this before and tried to copy them, but these, although similar, were of a different tone. They were more raucous, demanding, and confident. The magpie sounds and these voices seemed to belong to each other in this new place. This is what was different this time; there had been no other kids about when we were here before.

We were in Waylen House, where the boys around our age were placed first. I don't think our Coogee group filled this small upstairs dormitory, which seemed exclusive to us, with maybe only a dozen beds. It was a dormitory separate from the main larger ones, and at the end of the building that it backed onto; it had a door that accessed the residence of Peterkin and his family, where his children in those black, posh-looking school uniforms lived. The beds were end-to-end, with an aisle at the foot, and stretched the width of the building, with maybe four large sash windows on each outside wall. I would soon find out that there were many more windows like them in this place; this was no country post-house by the sea, as Coogee had been before we came there. The windows remain in my mind, and I don't have to go to Swan to see what they looked like, even today. My fascination with how things were made began around this time I would always look at objects as if they were meant to be pulled apart. They were solid, craftsman-built windows of generous width and height that let the summer sunshine in.

Only boys here; the girls who had been at Coogee with us were somewhere else. It would always be that way; siblings didn't matter in this new place. I don't recall my brothers here in this dormitory either, but they were here. I don't think I thought much about their whereabouts by this time.

Besides, I would soon find out that the minds of those who ran this place had very fixed ideas about the relationships between siblings and the sexes. Despite our eighteen months or so by the seaside, we were still Poms, as that call reminded me, despite our time at Coogee in the sand hills of coastal Fremantle. We had now arrived in the country of tall gums, magpies, a big, dark river and streams that would flood, and many more boys and girls. I remember going down a brightly polished wooden staircase we would get to know well with a rag and wax.

We were ushered down to meet the owners of the voices that had woken us. They stood in a rough circle staring at us as we arrived outside. They had severe and roughly cut hair, very short back and sides with a top tuft of hair, compared to our slightly more generous locks; the people at Coogee had forgotten how we orphans should look. All the boys were dressed the same, not like at Coogee, where my memory still sees multi-style hand-me-downs. These boys had well washed, worn, cast-off, bum-patched, short pants and short-sleeved shirts, nearly all washed to the same colour. Tanned skins and sinewy, muscular arms and legs and quizzical looks, but not unkind. When would we begin to look the same, I thought, as I looked for a possible future friend? Why the menacingly short hair, I wondered; these were not like the Aussie kids at Beaconsfield Primary. Then, Peterkin the Boss appeared, the man who would control our every step from here on. A name I had only heard spoken about before, but I had not met in the flesh.

He looked a mountain of a man, although later in life I found he wasn't that at all. He looked solid, with grey, close-cropped crew cut; he was dark-suited, immaculate and commanding. He had round black steel-rimmed smallish eyes that seemed to hold no warmth for us at the time. A long thick rod of blonde wood was gripped in his right hand, where it bulged at one end. It was planted alongside him like a signpost. It is how I will always remember him. The vision told me, beware! I had met the Boss and his rod. A whistle hung around his neck, one of those shrill ones. He used it for announcing his commands, as I would soon find out. Now I knew why the boys' hair was cropped so short. They looked at us, some with small smiles, but frowns mainly. We were a group of new kids, and migrant intakes were still a curiosity, a novelty, as we still spoke differently. Coogee had not yet removed that and our English look, for we had been alone in our own world still and mostly with our own kind, so we were alike, almost as if we had still just stepped off that ship.

Yet I felt no fear. I know now that we were the same as them, we were alone like them, and like them, some with brothers or sisters, but with no home with a mum and/or dad. I see it now, but did not understand it then. It was the leveller that made us equal in a way. There were bullies, I would soon find out; some came and went, but they could not hide from a type of group justice. No one was better than the other, and if one was picked on, everybody knew. Of course, some were smarter, but at this place called Swan we were all here for the same reason. The boys here were of ages from kindergarten to high school, and of various origins and inclinations, but with well-defined group allegiances that we soon had to learn to understand, in that childlike innocent way. It was all quite different compared with Coogee, where all ages were together, as I would soon find out.

It was the height of summer, January 1951, and as I was now Australian enough, I had come to a place called Middle Swan on the northern outskirts of Midland Junction. I would stay here for the remainder of my childhood, another seven years. I'd learn to become more of an Australian, even though I know now that part of me was as Australian as the rest of them, but right now I was still a Pom as far as these locals were concerned. During our time here, Fred would continue to write numerous letters to Peterkin. At this time, though, Fred was still at sea and his letters to Peterkin were mainly about Don, who would soon be fifteen, and his future education. That Fred was now well established as the active parent is also clear in Peterkin's responses. In about a year, in early 1952, Fred would leave his life at sea and settle in Perth. From those letters, I can track his steps as he established himself in Perth and the inner suburbs where he would gravitate to. All his jobs would now be in the hospitality business.

Fred's letters to Peterkin in this period paint a picture of cheerful optimism, but give no indication that he had any intention of gaining our custody at any stage. I don't remember him ever visiting me at Swan, although the records say he did. I get the impression that he was waiting patiently in the background and seemed to be focussed on establishing himself, waiting for us to appear out the other end of this Swan/State pipeline. He would find finally the money to fund Don's secondary education at Guildford Grammar, and my older brother's Leaving Certificate level there too. At one time, he suggests to Peterkin the involvement of one of his brother's Melbourne family in Donald's and my sister's future. Which, considering what he got up to before all this, was somewhat of a paradox to me.

Our grandparents would also write to Peterkin, their letters describing their continuing bewilderment and sorrow and pressing for news of us. They died when I was still at Swan, Elizabeth in 1955 and Leonard in 1957, the year just before I left. I didn't know that when I began this story. I wonder what my reaction would have been if we had been told then – probably little, by that time. I could not remember them; perhaps I was too young. Despite their obvious major role in our early lives, their deaths seemed to have passed without a murmur from Fred or Daphne or anybody else. They were old, but not that old; Leonard was seventy-eight and Elizabeth seventy-seven, and for both heart failure was given as the main cause. As a grandparent of that age now, I could venture their hearts were broken already – all their family gone from their lives – never to be seen again.

Daphne would also write to Peterkin, but less often, and not to us like her parents did. Her letters from this time show a cautious optimism that she would soon be reunited with us in some way. Reading them, it appears that she didn't have the means, and never would. She tried to involve people she established friendships with in our care. Her plans were always wrecked by the State. They come across as a stern, unbending, and ever present, remote authority, making judgements without allowing any questioning or recourse by parents or Swan. Every request she made was examined minutely for any indication she was unfit as a parent, as if she was assumed to be at the outset. Swan, although they were also ever present in our care, really had no more say in what happened to us parenting-wise than our parents did. We clearly belonged to the State; any question of who would take care of us other than Swan at any time had to be referred to them, and the bar was set very high and arbitrarily applied, with no allowance for a review of their decision.

After Daphne's arrival at the end of 1950, it appears that she began to work towards getting us back, whilst working in a familiar environment as a domestic in the Mount hospital in Perth. She first wrote to Peterkin in January 1951, so she didn't waste any time. It was clear she had plans to re-engage with us as soon as she could. She uses optimistic words that indicate that soon she would "have us back." It's likely that was the official advice she got about children like us who were not fostered or institutionalised kids from England. She soon came to see us, perhaps as a show of this optimism. Looking at hers and the State's correspondence as a whole, her view of what was appropriate and her belief that she could participate in what happened to us regardless of her circumstances was misplaced. As was her apparent belief that her private life would remain apart and didn't matter; it did, but more on that later. The odds of getting any of us back were stacked against Daphne from the start. Any stories told to her by Mrs Jones or Australia House in England, supporting her as the preferred parent during that time she decided to ship us off, were misguided. I cannot remember what I thought about her at this time – my life had started at Waylen House, in a totally different environment than before.

19

WAYLEN HOUSE

Waylen House lay in the countryside, surrounded mainly by vineyards, which we would visit regularly, though never by invitation. Swan's early history as a boys' orphanage is well documented elsewhere, so I won't go into that part of it; needless to say, it was well known, and not just in the main metropolis of Perth. Swan's Anglican parish champions travelled all over the State of Western Australia seeking charitable support, even as far north as Geraldton and south as Albany. This army of supporters were mainly lay church people. There were individuals who worked tirelessly to supplement our diet from the proceeds of local church fêtes and the like. Much of this can be read about in the newspapers of the time. There were open days at Swan when some family visited, including Daphne, on the only occasion I remember. They had a fête-like atmosphere and would be advertised in the Perth dailies. So, it wasn't just kin who visited us; as at Coogee, there were like-minded people.

By the 50s, it had become a large place by orphanage standards and had launched into building extra accommodation in community type houses, using the older boys' labour under trade supervision, and funded by generous local identities and charities. Of the line of buildings of varying ages, the recent ones were two large two-storey ones for girls and two smaller ones for little children, which all had self-contained bathrooms. There was a gymnasium and a communal dining hall where we all ate our main meals, with a kitchen and storehouse. The house where the older boys lived, Waylen, was connected by a courtyard to another building, the original boys' orphanage, called Brown House. In that building, there was another smaller dormitory, the older boys' communal bathroom, a boiler house and laundry, and a sewing room/clothing store. Brown was the first orphanage, built in 1868, and Waylen was built in 1903. They were built to house orphan boys, and had seen a lot of pain and mischief before we arrived. Beyond these two buildings and adjacent to the church was the one long building that I mentioned earlier, which the boys helped build. After that was a large, barn-like garage where all the vehicles were kept and the woodheap, where I was introduced to the largest centipedes on earth! The buildings that comprised Swan weren't that grim looking – a mixture of Victorian brick and stucco – but unmistakably institutional, functional, pre-First World War and post the second – you could tell what they were for!

For us, fêtes and the like were just another event that broke the routine of the company of a couple of hundred boys fighting for supremacy. At fêtes, we got special foods like pies, chocolates and other goodies. We were always hungry, but were fed enough. It was simple fare, and there were no fat boys at Swan. Always cereal for breakfast and tea in tin mugs, and dinner was regularly meat and veg and a simple pudding with custard. We had an occasional supper of bread crust and dripping as a treat. It must have been a sound diet as we were rarely ever sick or had toothaches. Our wounds were lots of scratches and bruises, given or accidental and that healed without any special care. I remember once a blowfly laying eggs in my stubbed big toe and its maggots cleaning it up. First aid was administered by a Mrs Parry, but it was rudimentary to say the least. It was a simple life, separated from the fashions and fads of society, and probably better than for some in other places like ours, which I won't name, where we would visit occasionally to play footy, mainly. But it bred a type of individuality that could not be erased in later life. God and the church were around us, but we were a soulless lot really, with very firm ideas as to where we stood in the scheme of things, young as we were. I can write such words about it now as I have a better understanding, but it is my adult view from a more satisfying life than I might have expected after leaving the place at sixteen.

I suffered mainly from headaches – was it the missing glasses? – more likely from staring at the stars at night and dreaming of what was outside there! The night skies at Swan then were all about the Milky Way and the Big Dipper and shone brightly every cloudless night, and are still a favourite of mine. The missing glasses were mentioned in a letter to Peterkin from the State. It asked if my glasses had been replaced. Peterkin said the glasses had been taken care of; but I didn't arrive at that recruitment place wearing any.

The State's letter also said I was "emotionally maladjusted" and in the wrong class, that is, a class ahead, and should stay and repeat and be given coloured drawing pencils "to draw in my spare time." Peterkin said he was not surprised, because "Victor had problems being the youngest" and referred to Fred and Daphne as the cause, as apparently I was the only one "shared between them" whatever that meant, and which puzzles me to this day. This episode and its timing remain a mystery to me, and the methods of the State curious to say the least. The State letter referred to a Beaconsfield school psychological report from 1950, and Peterkin was responding to a 1955 letter. But it does show how the State kept tabs on us; and that its processes somewhat slow to react.

Peterkin was an educated man; he had been to university and had a teaching background. I did not know that then, of course, but it explains my strong memory of him occasionally wearing what I know now was an academic gown. He wore it to church, and sometimes during our homework, which he used to supervise at times. His educational background was most likely the reason we had 'prep,' which was done in the dining room, boys only. I know now he was directly responsible for appointment of all staff. So, what about his staff; were they all like that caring couple, the Logans?

There was a couple like them, their name was Parry, and both had key roles, but the rest, to me, were a disparate lot. Probably none were educated in some way in how to bring up children; that's pretty well understood now. Such trained people were almost unknown in institutions like Swan in those days. As it was Anglican, there were no Brothers, of course … so, where did the staff come from and what were they like? Suffice to say that, after looking at the readily available case study reports from that period, it's clear to me that Swan lies very low down on the scale of the abuse of children during my time. Of course, I can only speak for myself, but modern reports based on incidents reported by some at the wrong end of the abuse show this to be so in a general sense. It may have happened, and I would never deny that. However, I never encountered anything but physical violence from big kids as well as staff. Boxing was my antidote for any of that.

This situation may have been down to Peterkin and his small, close-knit team of insiders. These were people, I found out, had been with him from the beginning of his time there. They were those who, I came to see, were his trusted staff, mainly women. If that sounds like a secret gendered network, it wasn't really meant that way. It's just that he had a couple of long serving, reliable female staff who knew the score and kept a watchful eye and ear to the ground. The leader, I believe now, was Mrs Parry, the wife of the cook, the couple I mentioned earlier. Mr Parry, I suspect, was also in the know, as his purview over those who passed through or connected with his kitchen was wide. Mrs Parry ran what you could call a one-stop shop which once was called the sewing room and was part of Brown House. It was where she freely dispensed bandages, plaster, and aspirin, and supplied us with a fresh change of well-washed, patched pants and shirt, combined with her daily advice on remedies for any cuts or bruises and other injuries we regularly acquired. Mrs Parry's place was well positioned in the boys' part where she saw all passing by. She and her husband served Swan all the time I was there, despite suffering a personal tragedy during that time in the loss of their son in a road accident. They lived in the oldest building, called Swan Cottage, built in 1836. It was where I first tasted pigeon pie; such birds were in profusion at Swan then, and shot by Mr Parry with his twenty-two, a rifle we always looked at with envy.

The staff fell into three main categories: those you liked, those you were scared of, and those you hated. Why they were there is too complicated to analyse and understand, but one can guess. Some cared and some just wanted a job that paid, and to be in charge and make their own rules. With no paper qualifications required, it probably ticked all the boxes for those looking for work in that still turbulent post-war period, with a lot of immigration from Europe. There were, of course, many more than I mention, but these are the few I remember who made an impression on me.

Mr Antil was an immigrant from a Baltic country and a war-torn Europe, who had probably seen it all and worse, and had a desire to start a new life in a new country. I found out later he was an Olympic standard gymnast. He would prove to be a great asset to the home and give much and be liked by all the boys. Giant swings on the horizontal bar in the gym were his forte and amazed us all. In the gym, where we gathered for many things and not just entertainment, like occasional film shows, were the means of erecting the usual apparatus like rings, including a springboard and vaulting horse – the latter not only had a gymnastic use, which I will come to later. We were well catered for in that area, largely due to his influence, I believe. He made the parallel bars seem a toy, and his teaching skills brought many a boy to become more athletic than he might have expected in such a place. I would watch him with my older brother, who became more than the average gymnast in his care. Antil, through his extra skills gave something more to our lives, and it was a pity there were not more like him.

Mr. Darcy, an ex-Swan boy, I knew only a short while, as he left maybe just over a year after we arrived. Before that, and after he left, he became a well-known champion boxer in the West. He had come back to Swan as staff. Why, I do not know, but I do know he came from a broken home, and what I read about him tells his story pretty well. Darcy got us all to put the gloves on, and although he was in my life only briefly, he made a deep impression on me, which lingered after he suddenly disappeared in early 1952. I mention him because he stands out and made such an impact on me, not that I enjoyed being in the 'ring,' but I suspect he gave me more self-confidence in a place where you really needed it to get through days when another boy would give you the eye and take you on for the fun of it.

He was probably in his early twenties then; he might have

been even younger, as his age was hard to tell because of his fitness. He was just a bigger version of one of us. I can see him now; medium height, wiry and muscular, and always it seemed as if he was going to break into a boxing skip. He rarely smiled and if he did, it looked like more a grimace. Sharp-featured, deeply tanned, always neatly dressed in knife-edge-pleated, wide, straight-legged, Terylene trousers then the rage, and crisply ironed shirt. He was not a man to cross, and had a fiery temper, which would be his undoing in his personal life, and one of the reasons, I think, he did not reappear, which was nothing to do with his behaviour toward us. He left suddenly and did not come back, although we might have expected him to, as he seemed to belong in the place. He was in his element; he could box as many ears he liked. His hands were his weapon, but I don't think he used them unwisely with us. I neither liked nor hated him; he was just the man I remember, who always said 'box on' no matter how defeated you felt, and I expect he used that tenet throughout his life at Swan and afterward. One can read about what happened to him and why he did not return in the newspapers of the time. It's a tragic story, but after all these years I learnt a lot from it.

There was Skipper Anderson, who was an ex-naval Commander and the man who gave us hot water by fixing mechanical things like the boilers. He wasn't a member of staff as such, like Darcy and the others, and did this work voluntarily. I know now he had a job at a hospital in the City. Peterkin wrote highly of him in his memoir. His only interaction with the boys was with our Sea Scout troop called St Marys, of which I soon became a member. I liked the dressing up bit and all the lanyards and white woggle and badges. But I did not know about what he did at the home then, as he was a distant figure to me, and I saw him only when we went to Bassendean Sea Scouts, where we stayed, played, and learnt what Sea Scouts do. Peterkin's memoir mentions much about Anderson and what he gave to Swan in his time and efforts, mainly with the boilers. He disappeared one day, never to be seen again. The story goes Mrs Parry pursued him about some stories the boys had told. He never bothered me, so I cannot say if it was true or not.

The only other that stands out in my memory was Mr. Ireland, who would play the songs from the 1955 film *Oklahoma* over and over, especially "Oh what a beautiful morning," to wake us up for more mornings than was necessary. I remember him as a character who always wanted to know what you were doing. He also dispensed corporal punishment readily. He was to be avoided in the showers, regularly bearing a bum-aiming strip of linoleum if you spent too long using up the Boss's hot water. I always suspected he enjoyed dishing out punishment.

A Canon Hamilton was the only major religious figure during my time. His death was not that long after I arrived and I can recall; I can still visualize his dark marble gravestone in one corner outside the church, as you entered by the path we all walked on two-by-two on Sundays, and the sombre mood over the Home when he died. But aside from the general events surrounding the church and going to religious classes, none made an impression on me and did not intrude on my Swan life. The church did play a significant role in our lives, in a sense. The Boss was appointed by the Anglican Church, after all. But there were no overt displays of religion, as the church played no part in our daily lives. I don't recall saying grace at the main meal, but we had church every Sunday, and the aim, I believe, was for every child to become confirmed before they left. I don't remember the names of the vicars, Thompson and Churchill, from my time; those names come from the records. St Mary's had a choir, which sang from a dedicated gallery overlooking the nave, but I was never in it, as I was tone deaf. So, I never made the Boss's choir for our many concerts, public or otherwise.

I can recall fragments about what St Mary's looked like inside, but all I can imagine now are grinning faces and girls beyond my reach in that choir, the altar and its adornments, and where the wine was kept, and the brass eagle decorating the pulpit that we had to polish regularly. I do vaguely remember bible classes in the north transept of the church, where I must have learnt enough, as I became confirmed, a rite of passage for a good Christian then. That's not meant to be cynical; church parades in my army life would always remind me of Swan, but for different reasons. And so, to a look at daily life!

20

SWAN DAYS

We were not entirely isolated from the world. There were day outings, and not only to play football with those tough State ward offenders at the Clontarf Home across the river. We went to the Annual Claremont Show on more than one occasion; it was mainly a show bag collection event for me, to make sure I got the bags with the product sample goodies we never saw to scoff down as quickly as we could. And I played with the farm machinery, where I learned to 'drive' a tractor – well, start a Massey Fergusson. Much to my chagrin, I would later find that a figment of my imagination, I could not know how to drive it of course. On occasion, our concerts in the Midland Town Hall were reported on in the local press. At these concerts, I remember a general burlesque type number about everything farm-wise that might have been inspired by that Mr Ireland, and missing out on a role as a shepherd I coveted. There was also always a one- or two-act play. Peterkin was an Arts man, I recognize now, and I know he thought highly of my older brother's acting talents and he was regularly given a lead role. At one time I was given, because of him, a part as a police inspector in a walk-on role, with around five words to say, which I muffed. I soon learnt I could not act as well as not sing. In these concerts there were also gymnastic displays, culminating in a pyramid being built with the smallest boy on top, where I ended up once. It was the highlight for the boys, a pyramid designed to collapse at the blast of a whistle. I don't recall any injuries from twenty-odd boys flinging their arms and legs out and collapsing in a heap.

So, what was our routine at Swan? The first thing that always comes to mind is that all days were the same; well, mostly. Days nearly always started early with a cry 'wet beds round to the laundry.' In Waylen there were two large dormitories on the ground and upper floors, along each side of which were two veranda dormitories with about ten beds each. There was also a ground floor veranda dormitory on one side. These verandas were walled in with fibro and glass louvres. One on the side upstairs on the courtyard side had 'problem kids' in it. Who were they – I think maybe the weepy ones of a younger age group? One on the opposite side of the courtyard was for the oldest kids before they were sent to Cornwell House, the farm across Jane Brook to the East. Once you got on that veranda you considered yourself top of the kid hierarchy in Waylen. There was only one other on the side below that one, and if you were in that one you were definitely at the bottom.

That bottom veranda was reserved strictly for kids who wet the bed. Those kids we treated as pariahs, and some pretty crude equipment was used in those days as a means of curing the problem. They used rubber underlay sheets and battery run electric shock equipment fixed to the genital area. Most of us didn't care much about the how and the why, as long as we didn't end up on that veranda. Needless to say, there were always candidates for it, but fortunately, never me! My first dormitory was downstairs in the main part of Waylen. I remember it very well – the routine of making beds and cleaning and polishing the floors with rags on our feet. They weren't the only places we had to polish; I can still remember those stairs. Lucky we had no possessions, as there was no private space such as bedside cupboards; that would remain the case always. Everything I owned, I could carry in my pockets.

After a short morning communal shower, kept short to avoid a likely strap from Mr Ireland to make sure hot water was left for the Boss and his family, we lined up for breakfast. Always two by two, out the front of the dining hall, waiting for the order to enter – our behaviour in most things was pretty well regimented, even going to church. Breakfast was usually cereal or porridge and a glass of milk straight from the cow. Directly after, if in primary, we would run to school, always in bare feet, down Yule Avenue, past what we called Parry's Cottage, where those pigeon pies came from. I would glance at the girls' houses on the left, hoping to see a familiar face; then, where Yule Avenue meets Middle Swan Road, now called Reid Highway, where a mass of cacti grew – the remnants are still there, like a private signpost to my past. After about half a kilometre, we crossed the Great Northern Highway and our school was on that junction's southwest corner. I don't remember girls being with us, so want to believe they were escorted separately, as they certainly didn't run with us going to school.

It took us only a short while, and when I look at it now, the whole distance is probably just over a kilometre and a half, but we took our time, and we did loiter at times. In winter, we would loiter near the Midland Brickworks firing kilns, willing some heat to come from them and warm us. These kilns were on Middle Swan Road facing the road, and looked like a row of mouths on fire. In winter, wet feet from the puddles and the cold wind gave us what we called 'the cuts' across our feet – chilblains, of course. The recommended cure was to piss on them if you couldn't get a dollop of Vaseline from Mrs Parry, which didn't last. We ran in packs, not so much by age or class groups, divided up by the allegiances we struck as we got to know each other. Except for those fêtes, we were always in bare feet. We even went to church in bare feet! Our standard footwear, only for special occasions such as outings, fêtes or 'Visiting' days, was sandals. We only wore shoes to high school, and they were taken off as soon as we got back. An image of me with Daphne and my sister, taken perhaps a year or two after we arrived, shows us wearing those dreaded sandals, our main special occasion footwear, except for sandshoes fought over by a motley lot at Sea Scouts if on parade. It's not a visit I remember and I don't know why but it looks early in my time at Swan. I look rather carefree and nonchalant in posture, reasonably well-fed and happy. Footwear aside, it is the only image of me with her at Swan that I found, and like the 'cuts' on the feet, the pain and that memory soon disappeared.

Middle Swan primary school was mainly a wooden classroom building with a brick residence attached, like many of that time; it was built in 1867. It was typical of early colonial Australia, but I remember it looked to me nothing like a primary school I had ever seen before. Even Beaconsfield Primary, a Victorian edifice, looked like it was transplanted from Romford. I am pretty sure Fred would have recognised Middle Swan primary school when he drove past on those earlier visits to Swan, tracking us down. It is almost a dead ringer of that one at Beazley's Bridge that he went to in St Arnaud. Fred would probably also have recognised the behaviour of Mr Rodgers, the headmaster who struck fear into all of us. If Rodgers thought you weren't paying attention, his favourite was a surprise attack as he casually walked past, whacking you on the back with his open hand, lightning quick, so it was totally unexpected. I don't know what he expected from such corporal punishment, as attention was far from your mind afterwards, but this was normal behaviour in those days, a carryover from Fred's era.

The school playground had a map of the world in concrete that might once have had water in it, as it was a pond, but I don't recall it ever being filled in my time. The water tanks, I remember, were still there, but I'm pretty sure the school was on town water then, and I remember wishing it filled at some time so we could float our boats carved from pine tree bark. Rodgers would make sure we knew where we were on it and what countries belonged to the Queen. So, I still felt at home in a way when I got to Swan, but it wouldn't last.

There were other kids from the local district, and judging by the class pictures that survive and what everybody was wearing, we probably made up about half of the pupils. Our clothes were very distinguishable, as we all wore the same, those identical shirt and shorts I noticed when we arrived. And of course, we were the only ones not wearing some sort of footwear. In one of them I can see the boy who became my best friend. Our lunch came by horse and cart, the one that delivered our breakfast milk from the farm at Cornwell House, where I would end up.

The year of the Queen's coronation in June 1953 I clearly remember and was signified by a medallion with a red, white and blue ribbon given to each of us at school. By then, we had moved to the new primary school just over a kilometre up the highway toward Midland Junction. This was a brick school of the modern standard style, more like Beaconsfield, built to replace the relic ruled by Mr Rogers, but fortunately, I don't think he came with it, as I don't remember seeing him again. We still went by foot; we just had to leave earlier. At the new school, our lunches were delivered by Swan's yellow Morris van, which we called the Butter Box – our ironic humour at work, as our sandwiches never contained butter. They were made always with white bread and usually with cheese or polony type-meat slice. Our jam was from quinces that I hated, and still do. The jam was always lumpy and came to the kitchen in big cans like kerosene tins. The sandwiches we called 'sloggers' because of the thick bread, and the menu rarely changed. To get our butter, sometimes we would take milk swiped from our breakfast table and put it into little brown bottles nicked from Mrs Parry and shake it as we ran to school so it would turn to butter to be spread with our fingers.

We weren't taught anything about sex at school, and certainly weren't at Swan. At Swan, sex and girls were taboo subjects. This isolation from social interaction with the other sex in a normal family environment was the cause of a lot of problems, I believe. My awakening came at the new primary school, when I fell in love with a teacher's daughter named Viviane, who lived down the Highway. I ran past her house every day, and sometimes walked her home, but my devotion was not reciprocated. It was the time I went through a phase of being obsessed by the female form, and I would draw a lot at school. In one of my early school reports from Beaconsfield, repeated in that letter about my missing glasses, my teacher wrote, "He has a definite ability in art – his ideas are original and drawings show life and movement." But the arts or art school would not be my destination as a career in life.

The separation of the boys from the girls was rigidly maintained, even between siblings. Going to church, the boys always arrived first and had to be seated before the girls appeared. Apart from our mother's visits, I only remember seeing my sister when going to church on Sundays, and maybe at the dinner meal, when the boys and girls ate together, but sat at separate tables in the main dining room. That's where the looks and nods were exchanged and any assignations set up. The sensation of warm dry lips, kisses in the grass below Lee Steere House looking across the oval to Cornwell House on long hot summers' afternoons, and one evening with a girl called Anne, always remain with me. I was approaching twelve then, with high school beckoning. But at least I was in the right school year now!

This strict isolation led to not-unexpected outcomes, and there was one such event I remember well, but not one I was involved in. As at Coogee, there were no fences between us or around us, which to some may seem strange. But all recognised where the food and warmth came from, and there was nowhere else to go, for those like me anyway, as any home was far away, and there really was sunshine and oranges on trees here. In fact, where we lined up in front of the dining room, there were more than a couple of oranges trees I remember very well, often laden with fruit we dared not touch. We were them given occasionally, but to get caught 'stealing' them might make one a candidate for judgement day, which was all about punishment, not god! Anyway, as I found out later from his memoir, it was one of Peterkin's mantras that his charges would not be fenced in, and that was why there weren't any fences around us.

In the late summer of 1952, when the nights were still warm and the late summer storms arrived … I only remember the whispers after the event, that is, the kids' story. Peterkin's account is in a letter he wrote to the newspaper. He says that a small group of older boys and girls met up in the dead of night and crossed to the northern side of the river, using the main road bridge, and one of them ran into downed electrical cables. The reason he gave was they were going to steal grapes! The outcome was one fourteen-year-old girl dead by electrocution and heroic acts by female staff. Stealing grapes at night! It is something I remember doing myself, swimming across the river and back, the grapes stuffed down my shirt, but only in daylight. And somewhere else closer to Waylen! We were just adolescents of course, en masse running wild with hormones, not hunger. An account appeared in *The West Australian*, like many other happenings at Swan. It was also reported in the *Daily News*, another Perth paper. The boys' 'brave actions' got a mention, but it was Mrs Ahern who ran Lee Steere House for the senior girls who was acknowledged after the inquest with an award for bravery. So, there was no hiding from what went on at Swan, good or bad, but it was mainly good, as I see now that was written up in the papers of the time. We did not see newspapers at Swan, and whatever the real story, it showed how easy it was to go where we pleased, undetected.

When I first got there, our means of mass transport for boys and girls was a slab-sided flat tray truck – something you might see on a farm. This had removable wooden benches and a metal-framed canvas roof. The roof was often removed in fair weather. It was a Chevrolet, or the Chevy we called it. I soon learnt the well-known cars and their slang names. The Boss owned a black Austin A40 which he replaced up through the models to that rounded A60 in the late 50s; I always thought the colour black suited him.

Davies, the Sea Scouts leader, had a light blue Ford Consul, which would be upgraded to a Zephyr in my time, both of which seemed to suit his character, and I know he might have shared the driving of his cars with the older boys at times, but not me. I only mention them because they serve as anchors for the memory in a simple and what was sometimes a monotonous life. We took notice of such detail then, as part of the fabric or landscape of our 'meaning of life' on a pretty blank canvas.

So, back to the Chevy; the centre piece of this particular event again involved electricity. We would travel everywhere in the Chevy, to high school, to Coogee for the Christmas holidays, and to the Perth showground, and sometimes, to those annual concerts we gave in Midland. It must have been quite a sight to see a cattle truck with a mass of kids of all sizes dressed nearly all the same, waving and calling out at times to sights that we thought funny, as kids do; boys only, as we never travelled with the girls. We would load up in a rush to get the best place near the sides. The Chevy would park in the lane facing the kitchen, just at the back of Waylen, between Mrs Parry's sewing room and an outbuilding that was a toilet block, with lighting of course; that same toilet block where we pissed on our chilblains. The Chevy's usual canopy was not fitted this time.

A boy called Bruno – well I am not certain that was his real name, but we called him that because he was big and slow, and in our boy-speak, that meant in the head. We were well nigh fully loaded to go and I was pretty much alongside him when he started to descend slowly, red faced, bubbles coming from his mouth. He had reached up and grabbed the power feed wires leading to that toilet block. A sight hard to erase from memory; I close my eyes and I can still see him now, frothing at the mouth, slowly descending in front of me to the floor of the truck. Fortunately, the back tray was still down, but it didn't really matter. The scene must have looked like when we'd piss into the middle of an ants' nest. There were kids scattering in all directions getting off and away from that truck.

Bruno was taken to hospital and survived his encounter with 230 volts, returning about a month later to tell his tale as best he could, and acting as if nothing had happened. I remember, though, the scars of burn marks on his hands. The Chevy was replaced soon after by an Austin bus with the name *Bluebird* painted on its side. The bus was financed in the main, I later found out, by WA Lotteries Commission. There was no press report on Bruno's event that I could find, like that about the so-called grape episode. There was, though, a press report on the arrival of the Austin bus. The main reason for it being purchased, it said, was that it was 'undignified' for older girls to be seen travelling in the back of a truck. We liked the Chevy for its carefree style, and learned to forget its shocking departure from our lives.

When I was somewhat older, we went on a tour of the southwest in the *Bluebird* – something to do with the Sea Scouts. I think it was to Busselton, where there might have been a jamboree, a word I did not know then. My Sea

Scouts memories are spread throughout my whole time at Swan. This was where Vic Davies, our St Marys Scouts leader, appeared in my life. Davies was not many years older than us, and carried the same carefree attitude to life that many of the bigger kids displayed. The times with the Sea Scouts are probably some of my best memories from then. That was where I fell in love with boats and the sea. At times, we sailed Navy whalers and the larger cutter on the Swan; the boats were borrowed from HMAS Leeuwin, where we would stay nights, just up from the port where we had arrived. There, we would sleep in hammocks and eat strange food out of cans. It was a freedom we could not experience at Swan. That, and the use of the boats, was no doubt organised by Skipper Anderson's connections. Those boats' planked hulls and timeless rigging style always fascinated me. That particular experience would drive much of my later life in that direction. Busselton would also figure soon, when Daphne came back into my life.

The older girls would also tour the southwest in that bus; the aim was to broaden their experiences, according to Peterkin. On our tour, we stayed at Bridgetown and visited the Gloucester Tree near Pemberton. We travelled pretty well south on my journey; I was probably fourteen going on fifteen then. I remember climbing that one-hundred-and seventy-foot treetop fire-watch tower, with its winding wire climbing cage. It was where I discovered my fear of heights, but that wouldn't stop me flying in my dreams. The main southwest towns were where Daphne gravitated as she strove to get hold of us, well me at least, and take me away from the hands of Swan and her nemesis the State, as the correspondence trail she left behind clearly shows.

Punishment for us could happen any time, depending upon the transgression, and was randomly applied if minor. A strap in the bathroom or clip around the ear; only the Boss, on the rare occasion, carried a cane, or that rod that fixed itself in my mind at my first sight of him. But there was another scheme for more serious offences. We called it judgement day – always a weekend event, occurring on an irregular basis, maybe twice or more a year. It was based on an accumulation of misdemeanours by those above a certain age. The reasoning behind it was probably to make an example of what not to do as older children, like a lesson in behaviour when you're growing up. When I recall it now, it was a brutal lesson. And of course, would not be allowed, even in the family home these days, and I doubt its long-term effectiveness – short term, quite another thing!

Staff collected a list of transgressors requiring some form of formal punishment, boy or girl. Information was compiled in a list, with the punishment against each name. Transgressions ranged from giving serious cheek to taking something not yours, even those oranges from the trees where we lined up in front of the dining hall, or breaking any of the hallowed 'non-mixing of sexes' rules. Oddly, fighting was tolerated: one usually ended up being put in the ring with gloves on, in the Gym, or in the workshop building where there that boxing ring was always ready for use, to sort it out on the spot. I can still recall the feeling against my face and the sweet sweat smell of well-used boxing gloves, worn without bindings. All ages boxed, from what was called mosquito weight upwards. I think maybe that definition of boxing weight might have been invented at Swan. I also found out what a Southpaw was early in my life. Later, the Boss's written reference about me to the army said I was good at boxing, so maybe I got into a lot of fights. Anyway, back to that judgement day.

On the chosen day, all the children in this upper age group were lined up in the gym, spread around the two side walls, boys on one side, girls the other. There might have been a third of the number of kids at the home, say around a hundred. What followed was the administration of corporal punishment in a very public way. In the centre of the gym was a wooden horse, the type you vault over from a springboard – this was for the boys' punishment. A name would be called, the offence and punishment read out, and the boy told to drape himself over the apparatus where he would be caned by the Boss. I do recall girls being there, but not put over the horse and not seeing any punished; but the grapevine said they got the hairbrush from Mrs Peterkin or one of the House staff later. I never found myself draped over that horse, which may have been more by good luck than anything else.

We did have other pastimes, such as hobbies; they were encouraged, but the wherewithal was pretty sparse. There was a room near the library in Waylen where, at times, we made rudimentary craft and hobby stuff, some from balsa kits. I remember making a Hurricane airplane and a speedboat. We only had hand-me-down motors we could never get to work, so my plane didn't fly or my boat speed across the Swan. There were volumes of *National Geographic* magazines in the library, and they were our window on what was happening in the world. But our weekend days, winter or summer, were spent mainly outside; sometimes we hung around the play area across the fence from the kitchen, alongside the road to Cornwell House and the farm. The playground had the usual basic gear, a horizontal bar, where a move that only looked like a double shoulder dislocation but obviously wasn't were a favourite; something I never achieved and cannot find a name for now; but it looked really grotesque. It was where, between weekends, we would hang around until bedtime was called. As evening fell I would mostly lie back and look at the Milky Way appear.

Spare time, unless we had kitchen jobs like slicing bread with a hand machine and potato peeling by a machine, was our own, and there were many places to spend it. We had football and cricket teams, but I only made the football team on few occasions – forward pocket, as I could run. I never made the cricket team, where we played on a concrete pitch with matting and where I failed to master spin bowling. The Jane Brook Bridge and the 'Archy' as we called it were our main playgrounds, all unsupervised. I have not made up that name, only how it might have been spelt, as I never saw it written down. It was just the name we called it. It was a small sparse forest of saplings then, and we used to make bows and arrows from the young branches; perhaps that was the source of the name. To get to it, you ran across the oval, by passing the bridge over Jane Brook that led to Cornwell House and the farm. The Jane curved around from the Swan River southward, a tributary where we had our official swimming place, making a natural boundary for the precinct, as you might call it today that was Swan.

Stand on that bridge over the Jane today and you can still see the group of buildings in a line, boys' to the right and girls' to the left. I saw it as just one big playground bounded by the Swan and the Jane. The Jane would flood the Archy on occasion, usually during one of those late March storms that were common at that time of year. The bridge that led to Cornwell and the area of the Jane nearby was one of our favourite places. We would try to build canoes from lumps of corrugated iron by bending the ends, like you can still see in old photos, but getting pitch to seal the ends was always a problem for us. It was there we also tried catching gilgie, the West Australian name for the common small freshwater crayfish, which, I found later, everybody else in Australia called yabbies. My introduction to a gilgie was standard for a pommy kid. We were told by the one in the know to stand in the water near the bank and wriggle our toes, while he would stand on the bank with a makeshift net, pretending to catch our so-called fresh tucker. We soon learnt never to be tricked like that again.

As far as what went on in the outside world, with no radio, newspapers, or newsreels, we did see the occasional film, cartoons, and Westerns in the gym. We relied upon what we learnt about the world when at school. It was in the gym we also learned ballroom dancing, with Mrs Peterkin playing the piano, but that was a rare event. So, there was some supervised socialising with the girls, but that was it. I learnt the foxtrot, quickstep and the barn dance as a teenager. The last always the favourite as you looked for your turn with that special person's warm soft fingers. I would not forget those dance lessons, and later, when in the army at officers' school, they would help me to pretend I was urbane and I knew how to treat the female sex.

During holiday periods, some of us were sent away with our family. Or some stayed with other families, organised by a cohort of people with a mission to help others in life like us. Many were just farming people helping out, or some were prospecting for farmhands, you only have to look at the other records to know what I mean by that. My older brother might have gone once, from what I heard. Tales came back of special diets and sometimes, strict religious instruction, so I didn't mind not getting that ticket to a short, temporary freedom from Swan life to learn more about the world. Peterkin's letters say Fred visited us occasionally during this time, but strangely, I have no memory of that and I know I never stayed with him for weekends or holidays from Swan. In the later years, I went to stay with my mother in the longer school holiday periods. There were three with her, I remember, but not exactly when; I rely upon the record to tell me the exact periods. They started in 1954 and ended in early1956, but were never during Christmas, just term holidays. There were none in 1957 up until I left at the end of that year. The record shows it was always a battle for Daphne to get hold of me. Peterkin would say I wanted to go to Coogee, or the State intervened. It is clear I had made up my mind about Daphne by this time, but I cannot venture any reason from any experience. It appears that I just lost interest in her. Harsh, I know, but I cannot explain it otherwise. That is probably why these accounts may seem dispassionate to say the least.

The first time with Daphne was in a mid-year school holiday period; she was with a farmer whose name I do not know, nor if they were married at all. It was near Busselton, and her maiden name had changed, according to the official correspondence in the record. It would turn out that the State found the change of name questionable, for no reason I can see, but I believe it was the official attitude of the time. I remember going to the beach with them, but thinking it was not as good as Coogee. Also helping the farmer she was with to castrate his lambs with a razor blade, and nearly running him over with his tractor. It was one of those common grey Massey Fergusons that I had played with, as I mentioned before, when we went to the Show at Claremont. Of course, I knew how to drive it – I was fourteen going on fifteen! I can still remember him swearing as I nearly reversed over him trying to hitch up a trailer.

The second was near Yallingup the next mid-year school holiday. I cannot really remember the journey getting there, but there is a letter she wrote and a follow-up cable that says she picked me up from a corner on the highway somewhere near Dunsborough after I was dropped off by a public bus. When I look at that now, it seems a pretty loose arrangement for a very young teenager travelling on his own. She was living on her own and had a domestic job at the Caves House holiday place in Yallingup. We stayed part of the time in a woodman's one-room hut in the forest nearby. I can see that hut now, smoky and clapboard-clad, tin roof, windows either side of the door. By this time, her surname had changed again, as shown in letters she wrote to the State about us. But I found no marriage record, and no man appeared when I was with her that time. The next visit was the last time I would see my mother for a very long time, although I wasn't to know that of course. This was the May holidays of 1956 and was in Margaret River, where I stayed in a house belonging to my mother's friends; she lodged there, according to a letter to Peterkin on file about it, where she said she was staying with people who were "friends of Swan."

The record shows she tried to extend my holidays at times and take me at Christmas time, but was met with short refusal by Peterkin, who wrote I had "other arrangements." As for whether she tried to take my siblings at any time I do not know, and have no memory of that. Maybe, by then, she had given up trying to get us back and started anew.

She did remarry officially, as I found from the record. All my other holiday periods were spent in the care of Swan, and at Coogee at Christmas time, and I only have fond memories of those, particularly at Coogee. At Coogee, I remember the six-o'clock swims and running up and back to the wreck again, living under canvas in a large marquee in the grounds of the home. I remember the sea journeys to Garden Island from Fremantle on the *Wandoo*, again with the Lumpers, and going to Naval Base jetty fishing for bream and trumpeter. I always thought that we were the lucky ones to be back at Coogee for the Christmas School holidays. I did not regret missing out on placements with family or strangers then.

Fred and Daphne seemed to fade from my mind at the beginning of that last year. By the beginning of 1957, I had turned that corner and reached a point where I saw myself as being on my own for good. And although I might have always felt hungry, maybe hungry for love as well, I never felt alone. Was the absence of Fred and Daphne in our lives when we were with our grandparents during those early England days the initial cause of that feeling – that I am happy alone? I keep going back to that early photograph of me with our migrant group, why was I standing on my own with the makings of a cheeky grin. The other large families like us are all grouped together. My older sister and brother are together, but Don, the eldest, stood on his own also. I certainly believe now our early life contributed to it in some way. Swan might have set us up for what was to come – not necessarily a good thing, of course, but it made you into a particular type of person. It was around this time that, mostly, any sense of family was lost to me. My older brother and sister and Don had left to live with Fred, or be in his care; I never really would. I wouldn't see Daphne for many years.

My life revolved around my close friends, who were few, and the girls I fancied at Lee Steere House. So, life went on in its simple way. We played footy and cricket and swapped cricket cards as barter for various things we might have treasured, like a favourite marble. Marbles and knuckles were some of our games in an otherwise toyless world. One time during these later years, I found some old comic strips in the library, showing Japanese soldiers in Australia; it was a story of invasion and it aroused a memory. I realise now that there had been the same worry about war that was fresh in my grandparents' minds back at Carter Drive. But I failed to recognize that then; there is just that memory raised by finding the comics. It was the same strange feeling that the sound of a certain air-raid siren can still awaken in me, even though I heard it only as a three- or four-year-old.

In my final year of high school, I moved to Cornwell House. Cornwell was less than a kilometre away from the main parts of Swan such as Waylen House and the dining room and kitchen. It was still, in part, a working farm, but we didn't work it; it was only where we slept and breakfasted. It was where our milk came from every day by horse and cart. That horse-and-cart smell, the musical clinking of harness and clopping of hooves will remain an iconic memory for me, always. Cornwell was part of the old farm where, first, older boys, then just the older girls stayed, until Lee Steere House was built for them within the main Swan complex. Cornwell was 1880s period and a pretty substantial building and was run then by Mr and Mrs Cope. It was the hunchbacked Mr Cope, cane in hand, who struck fear in all of us; but it was an unwarranted fear, He had a spine deformity, but from our ignorant viewpoint, it made him the more formidable. But he and his wife were caring people, I know now.

Mr Cope's remit spread beyond Cornwell house to all the parts of Swan, where one of his roles was keeper of the gardens, and roses were his specialty. A number of pairs of boys shared a small plot he assigned them in a row running between the big girls' houses and the kitchen and dining hall. There might have been about twenty plots. This was probably our only agricultural task. The era of using Swan boys as local farm workers was gone by my time. Mr Cope's garden was a boys' only occupation; the competition was to get the patch closest to where the girls lived, for obvious reasons. Although we seemed to be always hungry, we weren't allowed to grow vegetables. Border flowers like pansies and daisies were all we were allowed, and roses were definitely out unless you were directly under Mr Cope's special guidance. Needless to say, I did not get a passion for horticulture, and my main enjoyment was seeing things neat and tidy and squared off, which would remain with me throughout my life and prepare me well for what was to come next. What stays in my mind is the plot with the mature fig tree; I remember bagging that with one of my mates one season, so we had supplementary rations for a while. It gave me an everlasting passion for figs. What was it all for – a form of discipline and purpose in life? The notation on the back of the photo in this book showing this activity is maybe more apt. It says "Where there's faith there's hope. Where there's gardens, Mr Cope."

I spent a year at Cornwell and have only a few memories of my time there. The one dormitory slept around twenty boys and mirrored that at Waylen. Cornwell had a dark history, being at first an aboriginal mission belonging to the State. The building we were in was added later and was named after a boy, a midshipman, a naval hero of the WWI battle of Jutland; he had nothing to do with the place, but I knew nothing of that then. No history of where we were was ever taught us. Cornwell used to take the increasing number of aboriginal children who were stolen from their aboriginal families in the early 1900s as part of the Government policy at that time. I could not know then that one of the driving reasons I was at Swan, family reasons aside, was in the shadow of that awful white Australia policy that was in full swing, certainly in Western Australia, then.

From what I have read I now believe we were part of that effort to offset the impact of the stolen generation. All the children at Swan were white and nothing about the first peoples was taught or talked of. Any history taught or spoken about was strictly of the Empire and its settlers.

There was a small hall within the original building with an old upright piano I used to pretend to play. I remember hearing faint musical voices once when in there. The engineer in me tells me the ghostly voices of those other children were radio waves picked up by the wires connecting the speakers around the room, serving as an adequate inductive circuit with the right properties to collect some broadcast. But these days, I'd prefer to fantasise it was them, those young Aboriginal children of the stolen generation!

Near the end of my time at Swan, I had an episode in hospital, which I only mention because of the way it was dealt with. The State record describes it as something entirely different than what happened, which remains a mystery to this day. It was the mid-year of 1957. For me those later years were the best at Swan. Girls had truly arrived in my consciousness, but were still kept tantalisingly separate from us. We had moved to the new Midland high school, now called Governor Stirling. It was near the banks of the Swan River, but a long way from where we had swum with seemingly reckless regard. From it,you could see the playing fields of Guildford Grammar, where my brothers went, with that wartime hospital cross still on the roof of its main chapel. There would be no mixing with that mob though. Of course, we came by the Bluebird bus, which identified where we came from, but we had our school brown jumpers, grey shirts, and black trousers, same as the other kids, so we all looked like the normal kids. It was a much further distance from Swan than our old high school, and that would prove crucial for me.

It was just before lunch at my desk when I was beset by a sudden excruciating pain down below, where my newly discovered sense of becoming a man was learning all about the joys of life. The pain was so bad I fell off my chair; the next thing I recall happening was that I lay outside on a bench, where I stayed until the Bluebird came to collect us at end of school. Back at Swan, in the sick room at Cornwell, I waited. After a day or two, my left testicle grew proportionately with time. I think I was there at least a week before alarm bells must have rang somewhere. A doctor was called, and at last the term hospital was used. By next day my left testicle was as large as an oversize lemon. The medical records now tell me what had happened. Was it known of in young adolescent boys in 1956? One of the engines of my reproductive system had got itself in a knot, literally. The record describes the rapid onset of testicular pain leading to irreversible necrosis, that is, loss of testicle if not treated within six hours. So that was that. I had joined the one ball society before any procedure. Should the school have reacted more urgently to a collapsed child clearly in distress? Should Swan have been called immediately? When I look back, I cannot make a judgement on anybody. It was the time and the place, where the chances of anything different happening were next to zero. The fate of my left testicle was sealed on the first sign of pain. It did have some upsides, though.

I recall little of what happened next, until I woke to a raven-haired angel dressed in blue with a large white veil smiling at me. This was no nun, as she was wearing lipstick. It was the ward nurse, and a time when they wore those enigmatic, starched, white veils. I fell in love again, but with nurses this time. Another upside was when a doctor told me that my sex life was not affected, but I should look after myself down below in future. My first sex education lesson, at fifteen! That I could still have children would be proved right. Another upside was spending nearly a month in hospital. My hair grew so much, I lost that orphaned look. When I returned to Swan, girls looked at me differently. A Swan boy with long blonde hair – my day had come. Until the inevitable came and they put me on a chair for that basin cut we all wore to make me look the same as everybody else. The curious thing about this episode in hospital is that it appears as a case of suspected tuberculosis in the State and home records. Even the army wrote to Peterkin questioning the outcome of the "suspected tuberculosis" episode. I have no answer to that and there probably isn't a simple one. But – like Fred's, records are not always right!

As I had missed lessons, Peterkin thought I should join his cohort of brighter boys. Why, I wonder now, this interest, when there were so many in his orbit? Was this Fred's influence again, or Peterkin's recognition that my brothers had received special attention by going to Guildford Grammar? My brothers were probably schoolmates of his sons, so, was I singled out because of this? Perhaps, but what it does show is that we weren't just numbers on a list at Swan. A number meant funding via the State subsidy, which had increased by quite a lot by this time. That subsidy was important; the loss of subsidies would influence the future of Swan in the not-too-far-distant future. There followed, for me, about two months of six o'clock start, two-hour sessions of Maths and English. These took place in the carpentry workshop, that place where we had boxed till we dropped. It was time well spent. Peterkin must have seen something in me, as he made such an impact that my grades at the end of the year tell the tale. Maths has always been easy for me, and maybe I have him to thank for bringing that out. But there would be no higher studies or following in the footsteps of my brothers to higher education – yet anyway – Peterkin had that army scholarship for me in mind. He struck that spark in me, to look beyond what was in front of me and grasp what was higher up the tree, and I thank him for that.

At sixteen, my time at high school came to an end, and I got no certificate when I left. My time at Swan was over. I left with a renewed interest in the fairer sex after my hospital encounter. The knowledge that one of my engines of reproduction had gone to a hospital furnace vanished from my mind. I had in mind only the prospect of leaving Swan, and better things, like girlfriends, not so much male friends, as I had become what some would call a loner. Parents and family and their meaning had faded from my mind. For a while anyway! I could still only see clearly out of one eye, though, but I was headed for a military career. I still wonder if Fred had a hand in that, and did he tell Peterkin about his Gallipoli adventure? I know Fred filled out my application forms, as Peterkin's record shows he did. So, were they in it together? It didn't matter to me then and doesn't now. I was now on my own, well that's how I saw it, and I would continue to be without family for many years to come. Fred's influence on me whilst I was at Swan, I would say, was little. I have no memory at all of him ever appearing there, even though Peterkin said he did; it is not in his diary though! Neither are any visits of Daphne recorded in that diary, but she did come – photographs do not lie; old ones anyway. So maybe that is just memory failure but it is why Fred is not mentioned much in my life after I got to Swan. In my life after Swan however, when I think about what Fred got up to until he came home we I might have had similar dreams about what to do in life.

21

FRED & ME DAYS

So, what happened to my father Fred, that distant figure who hovered near us after we arrived in Australia? Who gave materially to our care, even though it was not required, and looked after my siblings when they left Swan when he himself had less than most? I met again that uncle and aunt whose visit to us at Swan he arranged. They were, I know now, part of a fanciful plan to take us away and embed us with his other family, that family that I am certain Daphne knew nothing about until she came to Australia. I knew all about that Australian family before I began this tale. Fred is still an enigma to me, despite what I found out. The boy from a country town who signed up to go to war, leaving home at sixteen, the same age and date almost to the day I did. Why he stayed in England, when he could have come home to his mother, we will never know. Why did he seem to project an image of success, when clearly, he attained no great heights in the world he aspired to belong to? I think the answer lies in what he thought he might have been. He did get very close to that, I found.

After we migrated and arrived at Swan, unlike Daphne, Fred lived near us and provided succour as we grew up. He stayed around Perth for the remainder of his life. He travelled nowhere else, as far as I know, despite his big family in the east and past history of claiming to have been to all those places; perhaps he had had enough of travel. Just as I have had enough of travelling now, having been to distant foreign places that included some Fred aspired to visit. He did ultimately take a kind of responsibility for us, which was unexpected, given his track record in family duties. I can only guess, and I hope it is true, that our disappearance to the land of his parents' birth was the final straw for him. He needed to go home, and our departure was the trigger, I'm sure. Our paths would cross rarely after that year I signed up. Fred would continue in the hospitality industry after he left the *Moreton Bay* that day in Fremantle in 1951. He probably left his dreams behind as well. He spent some time managing the bar the Claremont Yacht Club, where he mixed with the higher-ups in Perth society; he is remembered in their photographic records. I am pretty certain he would have excelled at that job. For a period he applied for and got the licence to run the Perth Airport Bar, where he was in his element, mixing with a faster set than at a city club or hotel bar. So he was more than just a steward or barman. There he made somewhat of a name for himself with his bonhomie, and the archive record shows he was a good tenant for Perth Airport.

After that, he managed the hotel Carlton on Hay Street East Perth, with his third wife, another Grace, but around his age. He had married her in 1959, the year I left Balcombe and became a real soldier, no longer Army Apprentice Bibby. This second Grace was a widower with strong family roots in Western Australia. Fred lived with Grace in her house in Daglish, a proper suburb and street, he would have said. I lived with them for a brief week or two when I was a private posted to an army workshop in Midland, but soon moved out to live on my own, as you would at my age, with girls in mind. I nearly became engaged in that period, but I'm glad I didn't. It wasn't to that girl down his street, the politician's daughter Fred wanted me to get to know. Although we did have a dinner date, and I still have one of those candid photographs that you would get sold to you on the spot in restaurants in those days. He made sure that that local politician; I can only guess he might have been the member for Curtin as Daglish was smack in the middle of that electorate, signed as referee on my Officers' School application. Fred never lost his touch, and his 'who you know' mantra has stayed in my mind.

The last time I would see Fred was in Perth, Christmas 1963, when I was a newly minted Second Lieutenant in the Royal Corps of Australian Electrical and Mechanical Engineers. I had just graduated and left my newly acquired white MG–A with one of my many newfound uncles in Melbourne, another part of that family Fred didn't tell Daphne about. The MG–A was more befitting to my persona now as an 'officer and a gentleman' than the old Hillman Minx – something Fred would have understood. The same Minx, when still an army private, I had rolled the year before on the way to Nyabing in the Southwest to see my favourite Rottnest date, a schoolteacher, my first serious girlfriend, who did not wish to marry a soldier. I was on my way back to Perth again on the Nullarbor train, all those stations rolling by, giving a wave now and then to those 'other people' along the track stops trying to sell me their art, me totally ignorant of their story. My Nyabing girl was long gone from my life, like the Minx, and I was also still a virgin, much to my chagrin. At Kalgoorlie, we switched to that memorable green-and-yellow-liveried WAGR narrow-gauged train that connected Kalgoorlie to Perth in those days. Its rocking ride and smartly painted wooden carriages with always crisp white sheets and wrought iron baggage racks are never forgotten. After breakfast, just past Northam on the home run to Perth, standing at an open window at carriage end, looking at the wheat fields scrolling past, no air-conditioning then. Warm, fine soft fingers wandered across the lintel and stroked my hand. 'I've been watching you along the way; I'm on a break from Melbourne,' she said and smiled; perhaps a year or two older than me. She was of similar height, slim, blonde, with smiling blue, wiser eyes than mine. Some small talk and a slip of paper folded into my hand.

I was headed for the Carlton Hotel to stay with Fred and Grace. I had nearly three weeks to kill and then back east to learn about being an officer at a place called Bandiana, an army camp in Northern Victoria, about an hour's drive east from where Fred's father was born. Next door to a place called Bonegilla where there was a migrant camp, still filling up, even then, with kids much like me when I arrived, but with parents of course. So, I would come full circle in a way, but still be classed as a pom, as I would find a few years later. I spent only one or two nights in a room at the Carlton at Fred's largesse until the intrigue got me and I made a call. I spent the remainder of the time losing my virginity. A red MG-TC loaned to me for picnics at Canning Dam and other places by my mate George from Balcombe and Officer Cadet School, and an apartment by the Swan River near Narrows Bridge, completed those two weeks of bliss with my 'Grace' – not her real name of course. Who she was, and all that happened then and why is another tale, and if perchance she can read this story, she will remember me I'm sure. So, those couple of days at the Carlton Hotel were the only time I had as a true adult with Fred; he didn't ask me where I'd been when I returned, and there was no fatherly wisdom that passed between us that I recall. Which was my fault, of course not his, this time.

In Fred's medical repatriation records that continued throughout the remainder of his life, his war experience is ever present in the doctor's remarks. As it continues from the war record, it's almost like the diary he never had. I don't think he ever kept one. One way or another, that brief experience of war lingered throughout his life; even his fictional malaria persisted as a medical fact later. The records show a level of stoicism throughout. When told to retire by his doctor in the mid-1960s, he is reported to remark that he still felt 'fit to work' and had yet reached 'that age.' As for achievement, for a man with just a high school education he did as well as any other of his kind.

I truly believe he accepted his lot in life in the end and made the best of it when he returned to Australia and tried to become a family man.

His second Grace visited us in Ipswich, Brisbane in 1971, where I was posted on returning from England with the love of my life. It was a real Captain Bibby that met Fred's second Grace. She came seeking a cure for throat cancer, which failed, and passed on soon after. Fred died in hospital in 1972 of natural causes. When I found out some time later in a letter from my sister, I was serving in PNG. I had a scotch or two and walked out and looked at the stars again, which shone brilliantly in the black skies common in that country then. Grace's relatives had allowed him to live in her Daglish house until he went to hospital. I saw no will and he owned no property in Perth that I am aware of, and I wonder if he ever owned any throughout his life. He gave his body to science and left only a small suitcase of his personal effects. No King's Certificate on Discharge was in it to show what had happened to him in that 'war to end all wars.' In Kalamunda in 2015, on the Anzac Day centenary, my sister and I remembered 1915 Pte F.J. Bibby 6th Battalion AIF. After the service I gave a booklet on him I had prepared to the local RSL; so he got some official recognition of his part in that war. I am certain he never marched on any Anzac Day, and I never got to ask him why. I had two sets of his medals struck with his name on the edge of each, just as he would have seen if he had collected his, and gave them to my grandchildren to share and keep his memory alive after me. There was no funeral or RSL service for him when he died, so I see this story as his memorial now. I try not to think now about what would have happened if his ruse as Captain Bibby had been successful.

Looking back on my life after leaving Swan and comparing it with Fred's I cannot help believing we were indeed very much alike. To me Fred was an opportunist as well as a dreamer. Apart from staying at the same London hotel, one surely has to agree, sitting at the right hand of an enthroned Esama of Benin Kingdom in his London Official Residence negotiating with the Israelis the price of a service check on his B747 Aircraft, and as a salesman visiting Istanbul and Israel, and Damascus more than once, could be called acting out Fred's Mesopotamia fantasies in a way. Staying at the Mayfair Hotel and getting bespoke suits made in Saville Row and on a family research visit shaking the hand of the Sultan of Pahang on his birthday in Kuala Lumpur, Fred's real birthplace, all would have made him smile. I imagine Fred in similar places that maybe he went to I do not know about during those between war years before he met Daphne. All that apart, doing all of those things I think is thanks largely to the boost Peterkin gave me near the end of that final year at Swan. It would lead to the completion of my high school education, to do tertiary studies and become an Engineer, and a travelling salesman like Fred. They were my choices, and so was becoming an Officer, and I don't really think Fred had a hand in giving me any advice on any of that.

Daphne I have treated in only a cursory way in this tale. But that's all that the facts allow, and this story is not about her really. I know even less about her life, but I mean no disrespect, and she did try. She did follow us, at the outset with our interests first in her mind, I think. I should say, though, that there is no doubt in my mind that our mother was convinced by the people from the Empire Settlement Scheme to whisk us away in a manner that seems clandestine at the least. She might have had the best intentions, but in the end, in the few years after she arrived in Fremantle, perhaps she saw the State and the constant presence of her nemesis in Fred too much to bear, and finally gave up on us to make a new life for herself without us in her new land. She did remarry and have children, so there is some solace for me in that. There is also no doubt that Daphne saw Fred as her ruination, from that brief account of him she gave to me after I had left the service, and back in PNG in the 1980s, when we had arranged for her to visit – a visit prompted by Don in fact. She probably blamed Fred all her life for what happened to her and us after the war. From what little she said to me about him, I could see that. And of course, she should also blame the State. There is a letter to Mr Peterkin on file from a State bureaucrat, written a couple of years after we arrived at Swan. It states that because of her perceived 'character,' and without any recourse, she should never have access to us whilst at Swan. To his credit, Peterkin ignored that, at least in my case. She died alone in July 2008 in her 90s. My older brother and I went to her Mandurah care home to attend her funeral, but sadly saw none of her Australian second family there. It had been arranged by a religious group who had become her family; she was with them when she had visited me in PNG. Amongst her effects was an electric piano; so she was musical. I made sure one of my grandchildren got that.

I have to add a postscript here that focuses on the children like us that came to Australia in that period post-war. It needs to be said, to put a certain perspective on the motives and mindset of officialdom of my childhood times, and why our speedy removal and 'adoption' by the State was so successfully achieved. It also explains a lot to me, now I am wiser and better read on the history of my father's land and where his roots lay. I wish to put the focus on that seeming flood of children from England and those with parents from war-torn Europe in that post-war period. The White Australia policy was still well in place in 1949 and race and the colour of your skin was still a strong social measurement of where you belonged in society. Although not so much a policy now, regrettably, it still persists in some degree in our society – an unfortunate trait of all settler societies.

When I read the shipping records, it was blatant in the listings of crew from Fred's time at sea in the Australian Merchant marine. In the government record, arriving crew, if not white were always listed as 'coloured,' with no name, just a number; and that was written in 1951. There were no mixed-race children at Swan that I recall; if so, perhaps they were white enough for me not to notice. But the mixed-race threat, as its protagonists called it, was still a question raised in Australian politics in the early post-war years, and a wave of removal of such children from their families, mainly north of Capricorn here, in full flow. After that war, there were some well-meaning people who had the interests of children like us foremost in their hearts. But there was also a broom sweeping up children like us in England, from 'broken' families or institutions. I believe that the Australian Government was firmly at the handle, with the aim of helping to reset the balance in this wider 'serious problem,' as the mixed race question was called, even then. Before I wrote this story, I read all of the books by the so-called 'black armband' authors and many others on that subject, including that part of the history of my adopted land when my paternal ancestors were the settlers searching for gold; all have made me believe this to be so. As they noted on our documents in Australia House in late 1948, we were 'good settler children,' and the process was swift, and the destination of Western Australia made much sense if you understand the history I refer to. Looking back on the whole story, it is only this that offends me or causes me any grief these days.

22

EPILOGUE

I didn't write anything substantial about my siblings in my part of this story because, as I have already said, my memory of them from that time is scant. This is my story and theirs is their own to tell. I hope my sister and brother will forgive me for that. Their version of events at Swan might be quite different. However, my eldest brother Don is the subject of this epilogue, because he may typify the many that were maybe old enough to understand a little more about the experience and impact on our lives of places like Swan. Fred ensured Don had a university entry education, and I wonder if Fred had urged him to do those law studies that he claimed he had in his early life. I don't know if Don tried, but I believe he started out in accounting. I know he soon went to Sydney and the music scene and all those things that provincial Perth didn't have for a young man in the swinging 60s looking for a gig with his own kind. Whether that was the reason he didn't end up as an accountant, I do not know.

I often wondered why I had no memory of Don from Swan. All I remember of his 'presence' is a nickname other boys would mention when his name came up – 'Beak.' Although my older brother says it was his nickname and not because of any facial feature, but I only want to use my memory - it doesn't really matter to me, but it underlines our separation at Swan. Most of us with any particular feature that caught the eye were given nicknames, like Atlas from our migrant group, for his big round face. And big, slow Bruno with his clash with electricity. If it was indeed Don his nose must have been prominent for that nickname, although early photos don't seem to show that to me, and when I saw him later in life it must have shrunk! He was there only a short time, and then he disappeared from my life to Guildford Grammar School. My older brother left my orbit soon after we arrived, and maybe ended up more than a year ahead of me in primary school; and as was the practice at Swan my sister was also separated from me. When that happened, they all seemed to merge into the greater mass of Swan children and so faded from my life almost completely. So I hardly had time to get to know them then. But it is Don who figures most in my thoughts now, when I think of Swan.

I saw Don's life as worldly in a way, as I know he travelled and once went to India; I wonder, did he know of Fred's aborted plans about that country? From some scraps of paper he left behind, he also went to Malaysia, where it appears he sought some answers that I addressed in my other book, that story of Fred's ancestors and gold. So, he too must have wondered where he came from at some stage. Don was special to me for that, and apart from his wide circle of friends, he gathered around him people who needed his help in some way. I know now he married once, but I believe it was only to help somebody from his travels, in a way that cannot be done these days. He did end up finally with a close partner from Swan for many years, who I also remember from that time, which may have told me something about him and how he saw life after Swan. Did something happen to him there and he ended up, like Fred, with a broken life? He always seemed happy to me with all his friends, so I don't think so. Unlike Fred though, he ended up owning property, so he did better than him in that regard.

There were moments later in my earlier life when our paths crossed, usually not by arrangement, mostly by chance. In our young adult years, I well remember one, a weekend on Rottnest with that serious girlfriend who did not wish to marry a soldier, where my gauche request for an overworked popular jazz tune in a night-time place there where he had a gig got me a wry smile. "Wrong song," I can still remember him saying, but off he went plucking at his double bass. I know now he was quite proficient with that musical instrument and had a wide circle of friends in Perth of similar likes; Daphne's genes there, I venture. Music has always been part of my life, but only as a listener, where as for him, I know, it was a lot more. Later, I would play one of his favourites, Miles Davis, to remember him by. I can re-create that first musical moment with him any time now and imagine him in a combo playing his music of that Sinatra time, a memory made that much easier with music. And, as a single, young army captain in 1969, going overseas, leaving him to look after my Brubeck and Sinatra records that saw me through the years of engineering study in Melbourne – just about my only worldly possessions at that time. A car was disposed of and a sailing boat I had built, romantically called *Clea* after that enigmatic Durrell character, sold without a care. Did Swan have that carefree outlook effect on me, even then? The army had provided everything I needed and I had few possessions after leaving Swan. I left behind, in army care, a small suitcase, the contents another not-needed part of my life. That seems ironic now after what Fred left behind.

The last occasion with Don was in his Perth hospital room at his approaching death, a while ago now. Don's centre of the world, it seemed to me, had always lain in Perth, and it was only during my rare visits there that we would catch up, alas, before I had the urge to wonder about the past and well before I had thoughts of writing this story. I had flown in from Brisbane and taken over the bedside watch from my sister. Despite the impression I might have given that I had lost all sense of family after Swan, we had all become closer as we watched our families grow, particularly in the grandparent years. Unwed Don shed his care and attention on our children as much as on his own wide group of friends and 'other family.' I do not have the skills to find an answer for that, but I think it was because of Swan and how we ended up there. I seek no sympathy or special treatment for our past and never have throughout my life. We all survived and made a decent enough life of it afterward, but it made us different than others, I will always believe.

I had been totally unaware of the seriousness of Don's illness and I still had expectations there was time, a faint hope we would perhaps talk about the past, and particularly about Fred. Fred had applied for and got an ANZAC Medallion. In place of the medals he did not collect from Australia House, perhaps, as I am sure he did not forget that place. It was another trigger that later added to my yearning to know more. My sister had given me the medallion on one of my visits to the West, and earlier in the year I had written to the army to ask what it signified. Their reply was further fuel for my wondering, as it referred to service on the Gallipoli Peninsula – something I had not known then about Fred. Anyway, thoughts of any questions were soon dashed as Don lay comatose, his body in a 'progressive shutdown' the nurse had said, 'but not in any pain,' she hastily added. I had seen him some months before at his house in North Perth, where he had one of those 'gatherings.' We were all there and it was the last time we three brothers had stood together, a rare event as adults as much as when we were children. It probably could be counted on one hand after Swan, like my times with Fred. It was on a stage affair he had out the back of his house, and I had wanted more of that to happen; it might have been his birthday.

So, in between the end of our Swan life and now at his bedside, I had my quota of questions, but I had left it too late this time, having been busy with my own life. I felt, not only remorse for the loss of a brother I did not really know, but also for all the lost opportunities before and during our growing up, which started in Swan. Yet that time alone with him might have inspired me to look more deeply, to try and answer the question: why did it happen the way it did? Then, I had yet to write about our ancestors to assuage that restless curiosity about where I came from, and then write this story to try and answer some of those questions about Fred and Daphne, brushing up against Don's life in the process. I wonder what Don would have thought of Fred's life story as I have portrayed it here; maybe he knew something about what he did in England and smiled to himself when Fred married his second Grace in Perth. I hope my grandchildren smile also when they read this story. And always ask questions, and don't leave it too late to ask.

ABOUT THE AUTHOR

Aged sixteen, Victor Bibby joined the Australian Army as an apprentice soldier, became an officer, did more study and became an Engineer, married, had a family, and saw more of the world than he expected. A second career in commercial aviation followed in which he saw even more of the world mainly through aeroplane and hotel windows.

As a young boy, Victor immigrated to Australia from the UK as part of the Child Migrant Scheme and grew up a ward of the State. Once retired, he began to piece together fragments of his family history, to answer the question: 'Why did it happen the way it did?' His search revealed a few truths as well as many gaps, pretences and evasions. The gifts of understanding and acceptance were his reward.

This is his second book and Victor Bibby lives in Geelong, Victoria with his beloved wife, a partner to the foibles of his upbringing and has four grandchildren.

Printed in the USA
CPSIA information can be obtained
at www.ICGtesting.com
LVHW090902241124
797473LV00005B/20

* 9 7 8 1 9 2 2 4 0 9 9 9 7 *